ASPECTS
of marriage

DISCOVER WHY YOUR MARRIAGE IS FAILING
AND HOW YOU CAN MAKE IT WORK

OGHENETHOJA UMUTEME

ASPECTS
of marriage

MEMOIRS
Cirencester

Published by Memoirs

MEMOIRS
PUBLISHING

Memoirs Books
25 Market Place, Cirencester, Gloucestershire, GL7 2NX
info@memoirsbooks.co.uk www.memoirspublishing.com

(c) Oghenethoja Umuteme, July 2012
First published in England, July 2012
Book jacket design Ray Lipscombe

ISBN 9781909020788

All rights reserved.

Unless otherwise indicated, Bible quotations are taken from the King James Version and New King James Version of the Holy Bible. Scripture quotations marked with NIV are taken from the Holy Bible, New International Version, copyright 1973, 1978, 1984 by International Bible Society. All rights reserved.

All rights reserved. No part of this book shall be reproduced or transmitted in any form or by any means, electronic or mechanical, including photocopying, recording, or any information storage and retrieval system, without permission in writing from the copyright owner.

Address all enquiries to the publisher;
Restoration Media House Limited +234-8092496045, +2348076190064,
Email: rmhltd.info@gmail.com

Although the author and publisher have made every effort to ensure that the information in this book was correct when going to press, we do not assume and hereby disclaim any liability to any party for any loss, damage, or disruption caused by errors or omissions, whether such errors or omissions result from negligence, accident, or any other cause.
The views expressed in this book are purely the author's.

Printed in England

ASPECTS of marriage

CONTENTS

INTRODUCTION

Chapter 1	In the beginning	Page 1
Chapter 2	Stages of marriage	Page 10
Chapter 3	The biblical conditions of marriage	Page 15
Chapter 4	The dowry	Page 29
Chapter 5	The spiritual implications of marriage	Page 35
Chapter 6	Why marriages break up	Page 46
Chapter 7	Sustaining the marriage	Page 60
Chapter 8	The case for men	Page 68
Chapter 9	The case for women	Page 76
Chapter 10	The case for sex	Page 110
Chapter 11	The case for children	Page 122
Chapter 12	The case for in-laws	Page 131
Chapter 13	The case for the church	Page 140
Chapter 14	The case for society	Page 149
Chapter 15	The case for money	Page 156
Chapter 16	Presence management in marriage	Page 174
Chapter 17	The case for spiritual marriages	Page 186
Chapter 18	Managing marital violence	Page 190
Chapter 19	Enjoying marriage as the years pass	Page 194
Chapter 20	The practices of divorce	Page 201
Chapter 21	Widowhood	Page 208

INTRODUCTION

This book will help you to understand why your marriage is failing and how you can make it work. It will also help you to know what to do when you are called to counsel a couple experiencing a failing marriage.

No matter how well lit your room is, you still want it to receive the rays of the sun at dawn. As you read this book, open up your mind to the rays of wisdom. Try to assimilate the wisdom this book has to offer, so that it means more to you.

God called me into ministry on October 19 2008 with the instruction 'Recruit, train and spiritually empower men, women, young people and children with the wisdom to execute my will on earth'. Little did I know that it would take me this far. To this day, I can see the hand of God leading me with a voice: 'This is the way, walk in it'. When the ministry started, the very first counselling I did was marriage related.

One night I said to God in my prayer: 'I am barely four years into marriage and here I am with marriage counselling demands staring me in the face. Where will I get the wisdom to teach them what they need to help them have a blissful marriage?'

While I wondered over this, I heard Him say to my spirit: 'You are about to write a book on marriage.' This was how this book started in 2009. First I had to send the wisdom out through emails, and I was getting positive responses from the recipients. After the email trials, I taught part of this wisdom in my marriage class for a couple that was about to wed, and I also received positive encouragements.

Then God brought in men and women who needed to tell me about the chaos they were experiencing in their marriages. My own home was not left out. There was anarchy in my home. I was wondering why all this was happening, but I kept on remembering what God said, that I was to write a book on marriage.

The knowledge came in like a swarm of bees. I didn't need to go far. The problems were affecting many of the homes around me. Women came to report their husbands to my wife. Men came to do the same. She would recount these stories to me later. Her suspicion grew any time she saw me standing with a woman. She had heard stories and seen movies relating to marital vices. She would hit me with a quarrel at every opportunity to do so.

Then one day, she phoned me to say that she had been enjoying our quarrels and that all of a sudden she had found

I wasn't fighting her as I used to do. No surprise about that, I was only testing the wisdom God had given me. This book is the result of these encounters; with God, society, children, men, women and in my home.

As I wrote the last lines of this book, I could see the hand of Almighty God stretched towards your marriage and His glory filling you with the wisdom to transform it. The Lord had sent His word in this book. Receive it, and see a broken marriage healed.

In this book, we are going to see what led to a misunderstanding in society today. The foundation of many marriages is wrong. These marriages were not made properly. Marriage has been seen as a certificate or a ring, a means whereby a woman can get a man to avoid the shame of old-aged prolonged spinsterhood. Marriage is not seen as means to uphold the ultimate purpose of God - to fill and subdue the earth with the wisdom of God.

As you take this journey with me into the world of the Aspects of Marriage, I implore you to be calm in your spirit, so that your inner mind can commune with the Spirit of God to give you an understanding that will project you into the realm of supernatural insights.

No more of this introduction – now read the book itself.

Oghenethoja Umuteme

Founding President/Senior Pastor,

Royal Diamonds International Church

(Christ Movement International Ministries)

Port Harcourt, Nigeria

For God, who instituted marriage, and to my lovely wife, Mrs Umuteme Adokiye Obele, for believing in the love we share.

CHAPTER ONE

IN THE BEGINNING

Marriage dates back to the Creation, when God decided to provide the man He had formed with a helpmeet. As a preamble, let's go through our understanding of what marriage entails:

- First, God formed man from the dust of the Earth and breathed into him the breath of life, so he became a living soul.
- Then He created a garden and put the man He had formed in the garden, to take care of it.
- Then God saw that Adam needed help. He caused him to sleep deeply before taking a rib out of him to form a woman.
- The woman was presented to Adam by God Himself and Adam named her 'woman'.
- The Bible went further, to conclude that there is a need for the man to be joined to his wife, his lost rib.

We are moving from this premise to further understand that the help God intended to give when He gave Adam a wife was to champion His course for man, to dress the garden God had planted. In the next section, we will be talking about the qualities of this help from God to man, so that he would not labour alone but have a companion who was comparable to him.

PURPOSE OF MARRIAGE

In Genesis 1:27-28, God handed down a command, a task for the man and his wife to conquer and subdue the earth with the spirit He has given to man, which is the breath of life. The man was to have a helpmeet of comparable status to him, so that one can easily fit into the other's shoes in actualising the vision of God for them. This is explained in Genesis 2:18.

ORIGIN OF MARRIAGE

As stated earlier, marriage is an institution ordained by God and dates from the time man was created, as seen in Genesis 2:18-25.

SPIRITUAL PRINCIPLES IN MARRIAGE

A careful analysis of Genesis 2:24 explains better the following principles governing marriage. It should be a perfect inseparable bond: The man and his wife are one, a united and inseparable entity because the woman was formed from man. In my book *The Man God Made*, I defined marriage as: 'an

CHAPTER ONE

erotic, passionate and inseparable spiritual bond existing between two unique persons of opposite sex, male and female, with a common destiny to fulfil, who had lived separate lives supposedly aimed at equipping them with the skills and wisdom that should enable them to execute the will of God on Earth, which is the common destiny they share.'

There is no way man can be complete spiritually without his lost rib. This was why the Bible told us that a man who finds a wife is a man who obtains favour from God. And this means that if our marriages are in a shambles, we know that we are not yet exercising the terms and conditions of the marriage union as ordained by God.

This favour is encapsulated in what motivated God to get a helpmeet for Adam in the first place. God hates divorce, which He sees as putting away (Malachi 2:16). I was shocked one day when I read in the dailies that a Nigerian pastor's wife encourages women to get divorced. Now let's see why God is angry with many of us, and the reason why He may have turned deaf ears to our prayers:

Another thing you do: You flood the LORD's altar with tears. You weep and wail because he no longer pays attention to your offerings or accepts them with pleasure from your hands. You ask, Why? It is because the LORD is acting as the witness between you and the wife of your youth, because you have broken faith with her, though she is your partner, the wife of your marriage covenant.

CHAPTER ONE

Has not the LORD made them one? In flesh and spirit they are his. And why one? Because he was seeking godly offspring. So guard yourself in your spirit, and do not break faith with the wife of your youth. I hate divorce, says the LORD God of Israel, and I hate a man's covering himself with violence as well as with his garment, says the LORD Almighty. So guard yourself in your spirit, and do not break faith. - Malachi 2:13-16 - NIV

Marriage is sacred

The book of Leviticus told us that divorce is granted on the grounds of infidelity on the side of the woman, not the man. But Jesus said it was due to their wickedness, which means that Moses only told them what they wanted to hear, and not that God spoke this through Moses:

Jesus replied, Moses permitted you to divorce your wives because your hearts were hard. But it was not this way from the beginning. I tell you that anyone who divorces his wife, except for marital unfaithfulness, and marries another woman commits adultery. The disciples said to him, If this is the situation between a husband and wife, it is better not to marry. Jesus replied, Not everyone can accept this word, but only those to whom it has been given. - Matthew 19:8-11

The disciples, who were right there with Jesus, seeing the manner in which He spoke and the seriousness he conveyed, could only advise that one must apply caution in getting

CHAPTER ONE

involved in marriage, because it is more spiritual than what we see: *The disciples said to him, If this is the situation between a husband and wife, it is better not to marry.* It involves vows. And we all know that we make vows to God, which means that the marriage bond is more of a vow unto God.

I will say that going by the standard set for us by Abraham, Isaac and Jacob through whom we were all saved, there are no grounds for divorce if the marriage was founded on a godly foundation. Abraham, Isaac and Jacob never divorced and no Christian will nurse divorce. Later on, in a dedicated chapter, you will see the reasons why divorce is not permitted by God, because God never divorces us even when we rebel against Him. We should do it right first time. Many couples marry all in the name of loving themselves, and later start finding fault, which seldom leads to divorce. If we know the will of God for our generation, we will do what it takes to salvage every marriage from being wrecked in the ocean of deceit, distrust, infidelity, gossip, etc.

One to one pairing
In older cultures, the custom of men having multiple partners, even in marriage, led to the acceptance of polygamy. As the Greek orator Demosthenes put it: 'We have prostitutes for our pleasure, concubines for our health and wives to bear us lawful offspring'. This shows that many early cultures did not value

the practice of monogamy. It is a heavenly arrangement that every man only needs one woman to help him. Otherwise God would have formed multiple women for Adam with the one rib He collected from him. This proves that monogamy is the original law of marriage, ordained by God. Every woman should therefore keep clear of every married man, so that they do not incur the wrath of God. This permutation is the correct and acceptable order; one to one.

The wife is comparable to the husband
In Genesis 2:18, God made it clear that the wife is comparable to the husband. This verse is self explanatory, especially to men and cultures which believe that the woman should play second fiddle in the home while the husband pushes his weight and maintains an unhealthy attitude towards the woman. Both partners should substantiate each other in marriage, socially, spiritually, mentally, emotionally and behaviourally. There is no order when the bully takes all, and every man must see this so that they can live a memorable life. Many men who are bullies end up losing their wives and children when they are older.

The subordination of the wife to the husband
Subordination does not mean slavery. Many women do challenge their husbands unnecessarily. Such women also fail

CHAPTER ONE

to bring up their children to an acceptable standard by God, because they often hide their children's ill behaviour. This is why in 1 Corinthians 11:8, 9, the Bible says: *For man did not come from woman, but woman from man; neither was man created for woman, but woman for the man* (NIV).

Similarly, 1 Timothy 2:13 says: *For Adam was formed first, then Eve. And Adam was not the one deceived; it was the woman who was deceived and became a sinner* (NIV). All this points to the fact that the wife must submit to her husband as approved by God.

Again, the Bible says: *3 But I would have you know, that the head of every man is Christ; and the head of the woman is the man;...*1 Corinthians 11:3.

Sex in marriage
Everything in God's kingdom has a pattern. From the way God created man and woman, I would suggest that the face-to-face position is the accepted mode of copulation. All the animal-induced sex styles will only breed dissatisfaction in our heart. More on this in the chapter on 'the case for sex.'

If marriage is honourable, then sex should be done in such an honourable manner. Dog style, for instance is for dogs, and since we are not dogs, this style in copulation should never cross our minds.

CHAPTER ONE

Respective duties of husband and wife

The husband and wife are to complement and honour one another. As God's instruments of peace, they are supposed to be dedicated to the service of God all the days of their lives, in love. As long as they are able to see each other as being there for the common goal of fostering a relationship that will honour God, the family will ever remain a strong united home for God.

Husband's duties

1. The naturally-assumed head of the house – Ephesians 5:23.
2. To love his wife to the extent that you can give your life for her – Ephesians 5:25,28,29.
3. Make her presentable: physically and spiritually, filled with the wisdom of God through sound doctrinal teaching and exemplary living – Ephesians 5:26-27.
4. Nourish your wife by providing for her needs. This includes good nutritious food, clothing to wear, and a shelter upon her head – Ephesians 5:29.
5. No matter her shortcomings, continue to show her love - Ephesians 5:33 starts with the word 'Nevertheless,' meaning that under no circumstance should a man hate his wife. Do not be harsh towards her – Colossians 3:19, 1 Peter 3:7.
6. Pray for your wife always – Genesis 25:21.

CHAPTER ONE

Wife's duties

1. Complement the husband as assistant head of the family - Genesis 2:20.

2. Submit unto your husband as it is fit unto the Lord, and not in acts that will provoke God into anger - Colossians 3:18.

3. Support your husband in the upkeep of the home provided he approves it - Proverbs 31:10-31.

4. Love him, and ensure he does the will of God. Pray for him so that he will have the strength to succeed in life.

5. Love your children and help them to succeed. Sarah defended her son Isaac against Ishmael's presumed threat towards Isaac. Hagar also took her son with her even in her discomfort, until the angel of the Lord visited her. Rebecca helped Jacob to succeed. Solomon's mother reminded King David of his promise to enthrone Solomon as King. Mary, the mother of Jesus, was about Jesus even at Golgotha.

These duties explain why husbands and wives must see themselves as intercessors and present themselves as holy vessels unto God so that they can succeed together, else the devil will knock them down with his deceitful tongue.

CHAPTER TWO

STAGES OF MARRIAGE

We are going to discuss the stages of marriage. A time comes when everyone will know that they need a partner to help complement their efforts. Even if we seem not to bother, suddenly everyone around us becomes uneasy because we are single. The stages I have outlined are below.

Maturity
Maturity is not about age or grey hairs, it lies in the level of knowledge acquired over the years relating to a specific aspect of learning. This knowledge leads to understanding when the subject matter resonates in our thoughts. Even at this, one cannot yet claim that he/she is matured; the knowledge has to be applied to solve related problems before one can claim to have climbed the ladder of maturity. As it relates to marriage, a matured mind seeking to become married has to first see that with marriage, the ugly part(s) of his/her life will receive beautification through the help of the spouse, meaning that

the spouse must have ascended a specific ladder of maturity in the specified character/attribute of improvement.

Defining qualities
To me this is when a marriage class should begin for all young men and women planning to get married. This will help them to know what they are looking for in a partner.

The search
With the already defined qualities, the intending young man goes ahead, with God on his side, to search for the woman who would be his wife. I am not comfortable with ladies searching for husbands. I would advise them to find favour with God, and a husband will come to find them. If God is involved, there will be no mistakes or regrets.

This is not an easy task unless the Lord guides you. Beauty is the first point of attraction, but it soon fades, giving way to the attributes of the individual lady, those that last. This is the undefined memory that must be left behind in the mind of the man. And this has to do with what makes that lady unique compared to every other woman the man had seen before. This is what we call a lasting impression. Remember the man is looking for a problem solver. There is a gap in his life that he wants to fill, so that he can move forward.

CHAPTER TWO

Obtaining God's favour
God is the originator of marriage, and He ordained it for His glory. This is why we need to seek His favour in whatever we do. Proverbs 18:22 says that anyone who is in a marriage enjoys the favour of the Lord. This is only possible when the marriage is constituted according to His commandment.

Seeking her hand in marriage
This is where the young man meets the parents of the young woman. Once both parents give their consent the first stage is achieved. The next person to give his consent would be the lady's spiritual father, her pastor. Negligence on the side of the pastor can brew physical stagnation. On the spiritual side, this is when the young man meets with the church prayer team to ensure that every spiritual marriage that the young woman or man may have been into is broken. The evidence of spiritual husbands and wives can be obtained from their dreams and God's revelations to the pastor of the prayer team.

Honouring God
We honour God in our marriage unions when we come to seal the marriage bond at His altar. Here God's servants dedicate the marriage to God, and He becomes a witness to the marriage vows. If there was anything wrong with a traditional marriage, as happened to Jacob, coming into the presence of

God and dedicating the marriage union to Him will ensure that the marriage is preserved.

A special thanksgiving ceremony should be organised by the newly-wedded couple to honour God before everyone present, and once again, the marriage is re-dedicated.

Marriage training
Many couples go home and relax after the marriage ceremony without giving concern to the infiltration of the enemy into their homes, because of their inexperience. This is where the experiences of others come into play. This is when the newly-wedded couple should seek ways of growing in the wisdom of God, and be spiritually informed. Attendance of marriage seminars will also help, but they must ensure that they receive sound doctrinal lessons. Many marriage counsellors want to be popular among those who attend their seminars and not because they have the wisdom of God at heart. I have read marriage books written with devil's intent in the heart of the writer. For instance, when such speakers claim that anal sex, oral sex, and watching porn movies by couples is acceptable. This is demonic deception. Adam and Eve never did such things, even after their sin.

Passing the acid test
This happens after the first quarrel. There is every possibility

that both will blame each other, and then blame themselves for ever getting married. They may even blame it on their parents, friends, pastor etc. These are all litmus paper tests.

Building trust
After the first quarrel, there is the need to start building trust. This is where many marriages start disintegrating. When we fail to build trust for each other, hatred and unforgiveness sets in. The woman may become desperate over many things if she is yet to give birth to a child, or if she is in need of a son. Distrust is the number one factor that breaks a marriage, especially when either or both partners start to see prophets and witch doctors to find out why the house is not seeing peace. This will further degenerate into the witch-hunting of in-laws.

CHAPTER THREE

THE BIBLICAL CONDITIONS OF MARRIAGE

The Bible remains the gold standard for accepting that a marriage was actually constituted rightly and godly.

Prohibited marriages
In the Bible we would read that some marriage was prohibited: *No one born of a forbidden marriage nor any of their descendants may enter the assembly of the LORD, not even in the tenth generation.* - Deuteronomy 23:2.

What this tells us is that not every marriage is acceptable unto God. For those of us who are already married, we should begin to question the spiritual and godly authenticity of the marriage we have entered into. Here such people are not permitted to enter into the congregation of the Lord, because the prayer of a sinner is an abomination.

Between an Israelite and a non-Israelite this prohibition was on three levels:
a. Total prohibition in regard to the Canaanites on both the

male and female. *So Isaac called for Jacob and blessed him. Then he commanded him: 'Do not marry a Canaanite woman.* - Deuteronomy 28:1.

b. Total prohibition on the side of the male in regard to the Ammonites and Moabites (descendants of Lot): *No Ammonite or Moabite or any of their descendants may enter the assembly of the LORD, not even in the tenth generation.* - Deuteronomy 23:3

c. Temporary prohibition on the side of the males in regard to the Edomites and Egyptians: *Do not despise an Edomite, for the Edomites are related to you. Do not despise an Egyptian, because you resided as foreigners in their country. The third generation of children born to them may enter the assembly of the LORD.* - Deuteronomy 23:7-8.

Marriages with females referred to in 'c' above were regarded as legal. This may be because the Edomites were Esau's descendants, and Joseph married an Egyptian. Jacob had also blessed the children of Joseph, who had an Egyptian mother. It was taboo and illegal for Israelites to marry non-Israelites, and their children were seen as bastards, as we can see from Deuteronomy 23:2. This is all the more reason why a believer marrying an unbeliever is not really a healthy marriage.

CHAPTER THREE

Between an Israelite and one of his own community.
This could be seen in our present dispensation as marriage between a brother and a sister of different churches, eg between a Pentecostal and a Catholic etc. In Israel, the regulations relative to marriage between Israelites were based on considerations of relationship and sex. In Leviticus 18:6-18 we can relate to these facts of prohibition.

General prohibition against marriage between a man and the 'flesh of his flesh'.
Special prohibitions against marriage with a mother, stepmother, sister or half-sister (born at home or abroad), granddaughter, aunt (blood relation on either side or by marriage on the father's side), daughter-in-law, brother's wife, stepdaughter, wife's mother, step-granddaughter or wife's sister during the lifetime of the wife.

In Deuteronomy 26:5-9 a special exception was made in favour of marriage with a brother's wife in the event of his having died childless. In some African cultures, the widow is sometime obligated to marry a brother-in-law in the event of the death of her husband, to remain in the family. This is, however, not a practice that would be accepted by believers in the light of respecting one's brother's nakedness.

CHAPTER THREE

Qualities of the spouse - the would-be wife

The legal rights of the wife are mentioned in Exodus 21:10, under the three headings of food, raiment, and duty of marriage or conjugal rights. This emphasis places the onus on the parents to have their daughters well trained. They should also learn a trade that they can apply to earn an income. Today, however, many young ladies have not being trained to exercise the duties of a wife. The wife must be comparable to her husband, and both of them must have the qualities of the Man God Made. See my book *The Man God Made* to learn about these qualities and get used to them.

Qualities of the spouse - the would-be husband

With reference to the same, the bridegroom must have what it takes to take care of his home. He should be a man who must be in charge, not as an oppressor, but as a revivalist, who must point his family to God, in his acts and decisions (Genesis 18:18-19). He must be a man who can comfortably feed his children (1 Timothy 5:8). He must be a man who can defend his family against spiritual intruders. He must be a man who desires the seven spirits of God (Isaiah 11:2). I also prefer the man who has been trained in a trade which he can apply to earn an income.

He should be a man who spends time with his family. In Deuteronomy 24:5 the Bible tells us that God orders that a newly married man should be exempted from war, or any public business which might draw him away from his wife's attention, for the space of one year. It may be that failure to observe this was the reason Uriah lost his wife and his life after David had slept with her. A similar privilege was granted to the man who was 'betrothed' in Deuteronomy 20:7.

Whose consent?
The selection of the bride is the most important aspect of the marriage process, because this is the foundation of a new generation to be raised unto God. If this is not done right, there will be chaos throughout the couple's married life, and in most cases, in the lives of the children born from that marriage. Bridal selection is usually not the decision of the bridegroom himself, but of his relations or a friend deputed by the bridegroom for this purpose, as in the case of Isaac. Even when a bridegroom had found a suitable bride, he still sought the consent of his trusted relative or friend before going ahead with a proposal. The ideal way would be to seek the face of God after examining the physical characteristics of the proposed bride.

Even at that, some brides hide their innate characters, which they know would drive away their suitors, until they are finally settled with the man. The maiden's consent is sometimes sought too (Genesis 24:58), though this was recorded in the Bible as having been done after the earlier consent of the father and the adult brothers (Genesis 24:51; 34:11). Whatever it takes to select the wife was left in the hands of a friend in some cases.

Betrothal
Once the selection was made, it was followed by the support of a friend or legal representative, as a formal proceeding undertaken on the part of the bridegroom and by the parents (especially the father) on the part of the bride. This was done under oaths or vows. This is what is termed the engagement night. The bridegroom gives presents to his future bride. At this point, he is not supposed to have any sexual relations with the bride, unlike what we see today, where an engagement ring in the hand of a suitor works like a remote control that throws many girls' legs wide open.

Engagement concludes the betrothal process, as with Mary and Joseph, the parents of Jesus. The bridegroom places a ring on the bride's middle finger, which is the longest finger. The Bible sees the ring as a token of the groom's faithfulness to the bride from the point of betrothal (Genesis 41:42) and hence, the bride becoming a member of the groom's family (Luke 15:25).

In the Isoko-speaking tribe of Nigeria, where I hail from, the betrothal act was carried out in most cases on behalf of the bridegroom, and would be followed with a family feast.

CHAPTER THREE

This act is frowned on by the present generation of youths, who believe they have to make their own choice of whom their spouse should be.

I have found that trying to sideline parents and pastors from the selection process is the reason for many broken marriages today. People enter into marriage under the shadow of infatuation. Later they discover that they are incompatible, and would start to change their lives to suit each other, until they probably start living under a pretence.

The selection process is too critical, both spiritually and physically, to be done in a hurry. There should be no attachment of sympathy on both sides, and no bride should accept the hand of a man who forcefully takes away her virginity through rape. Such a man should be shown the tough side of the law. Marriage is more than sex.

Neither should a man base his selection on a female's physical attractions, as many young ladies now use breast enhancement bras to entice men.

I think spouses could start seeing each other and consummate the marriage once the betrothal is done, involving the parties, especially the father and the pastor of both, as explained above. My opinion is based on the fact that Mary, the mother of Jesus, became pregnant after the betrothal process and was nowhere was it said that the actual marriage took place after she gave birth to Jesus, yet the Bible recognised her as the wife of Joseph, and Joseph was seen as the father of Jesus. Even the Angel of the Lord referred to Mary as Joseph's wife (Matthew 1:20). The Bible also recorded that Mary had other children.

We also find this approval in the case of Jacob's marriage to Rachael, who started having children before the seven years agreed by the father-in-law had elapsed. And in her case, it was nowhere written that there was a special marriage ceremony.

The marriage
In some instances in the Bible, before the actual marriage night, the would-be wife stays with her friends and an elected friend of the future husband becomes more of a messenger and is in charge of ensuring communication between the two. This is what John the Baptist referred to as 'friend of the bridegroom' in John 3:29: *The bride belongs to the bridegroom. The friend who attends the bridegroom waits and listens for him, and is full of joy when he hears the bridegroom's voice* (NIV).

However, I have also heard stories of how a bride became pregnant by a friend of the bridegroom during this period. Such an act is a reflection of the sort of life many of us now live.

At this point, the bride is regarded as the wife of her future husband; hence faithlessness on her part was punishable with death (Deuteronomy 22:23, 24), and as such the husband can decide to divorce her (Deuteronomy 24:1; Matthew 1:19).

CHAPTER THREE

The overall purpose of the actual marriage is to ensure that she is no longer under the control of her parents, but of her future husband. The bridegroom dresses for the occasion by putting on a festive dress, and he places a nuptial turban, much decorated, on his head, as a mark of maturity and leadership, as he will soon manage a family of his own (Psalms 45:8; Songs 4:10, 11). The bride dresses in white robes and wears a veil to signify that she is still a virgin. This culture was what prompted John's interpretation of his vision in Revelation 19:8, because it was a commonplace event which he was used to.

The book of Psalms 45:8, 13 & 14 reveals further that sometimes the bride's dress was embroidered with gold thread and covered with perfumes. The beautification process, apart from what the Bible says in the book of Esther 1 & 2, is still practised in many cultures all over the world, and I am sure you are aware how the bride is treated to be adored on the wedding day too. The book of Isaiah 61:10 and Revelation 21:2 demonstrate that the bride also wears a set of jewels.

The main marriage event starts in the evening. The wedding at Cana which our Lord attended was also in the evening. I remember growing up and seeing the bridegroom and his friends getting ready for the dance party. The following seems to be the procession order recorded in the Bible.

From the story of Samson we would see the groomsmen

CHAPTER THREE

or his companions (Judges 14:11), accompanying the groom, setting forth from his house. This is followed by the 'children of the bride-chamber', as seen in Matthew 9:15.

A band of musicians or singers performs behind for the groom to dance in celebration while waiting for his bride (Genesis 31:27; Jeremiah 7:34, 16:9). This is normally accompanied by trained persons hearing flaming torches (Jeremiah 25:10, Matthew 25:7, Revelation 18:23).

The hallmark of the event is when the groom takes the bride with her friends to his abode, where a feast is prepared, to which all are invited (Genesis 29:22, Matthew 22:1-10, Luke 14:8, John 2:2) and the merriment is extended to seven or even fourteen days (Judges 14:12, Job 8:19).

The invited guests were dressed with fitting robes provided by the host, and those who were not dressed properly in the robes were asked to leave the feast (Matthew 22:11). Occasionally, as in the case of Samson and Delilah, the guest would be treated to an entertainment session featuring jokes, riddles and short stories (Judges 14:12).

Today, in other cases, a special guest would read Bible passages to encourage the newly-weds at the reception, as is done in many Christian marriages, though they are celebrated in the daytime.

The marriage consummation is the last act everyone will be expecting. This ceremony involves the conducting of the bride to the bridal chamber (Judges 15:1, Joel 2:16, Psalms 19:5, Joel 2:16). The bride was still completely veiled at this point, which could be the reason why Jacob didn't know that the woman he was lying with was not Rachael (Genesis 29:23).

From records in the Bible, it would seem that the actual marriage ceremony could take place up to a year from the day the betrothal was celebrated (Genesis 24:55). For widows, it could take up to a month, which may not have allowed her enough time to get over the death of their husband, as could be seen in the case of Abigail. Though there is no special Biblical law regulating this, once the betrothal is done it is necessary that the marriage is done on time to prevent sexual temptation.

Exceptional Cases

In exceptional cases for matured adults the marriage process may not follow any firm rule, as in the case of Abigail's marriage to King David, where Abigail had to accept David as her husband without due traditional diligence. Ruth's marriage to Boaz was another exception, where the woman had to be the one seeking the man. And again, unlike many cases where the family of the bridegroom must accept the bride before she can become the wife, Moses alone went to take his wife.

This may not be unconnected with the disregard Miriam had for Zipporah. If God accepted Zipporah's intervention to save Moses' life, then she was accepted as a priestess of God.

CHAPTER THREE

This is why a pastor's wife has a spiritual obligation to act as associate pastor to her husband. If Zipporah interceded for her husband, a man of honour before God, then she also interceded for the entire nation of Israel which Moses was sent to bring to God. Without her intervention, that rescue mission would have been cut short by the death of Moses.

The place of upbringing and societal values
The wife to be must have exercised an important influence in her own home, as she learned under her mother who should have been cultured as an elder. The Bible says that the elder women should teach the young women to be sober, to love their husbands and to love their children (Titus 2:4). I would say that this process should be documented, and the approval of the trainer should be sought. In this way young women would be prepared for marriage on time.

But do we really have older women who have the wisdom of God in them these days, as shown in Titus 2:3? A woman must have taken part in the overseeing of her family affairs, and should have enjoyed a considerable amount of independence in cooking and attending to guests (Judges 4:18; 1 Samuel 25:14; 2 Kings 4:8) etc. The importance of the characters and values of both spouses in mutual relationships are a subject of frequent exhortation in the New Testament (Ephesians 5:22-33, Colossians 3:18-19, Titus 2:4-5, 1 Peter 3:1-7).

CHAPTER THREE

The Biblical duties of the wife in the household were varied; in addition to the general overseeing of the domestic chores, which also include cooking, no matter her status (Genesis 18:8, 2 Samuel 13:5), the distribution of food at meal times (Martha – Luke 10:40), and the manufacture of the clothing and of the various fabrics required in her home (Proverbs 31:10-31). If she were a model of activity and skill, she would produce a surplus of fine linen shirts and girdles, which she would sell and so, like a well-freighted merchant ship, bring wealth to her husband from afar. All these are seen as the qualities of a virtuous woman (Proverbs 31:10-24).

The book of Proverbs 14:1 lays emphasis on the wife's responsibility to build the home. For her to do this onerous task, she has to be trained early enough. This is lacking in our present dispensation, and many marriages are heading towards collision as surely as the *Titanic* steamed towards the iceberg.

Cohabitation

It has become popular for male and female to live together. Cohabitation involves two people who are not married living together in an intimate sexual and emotional relationship. It should not be encouraged by Christians because it has the following dangers:
- Insecurity on the side of the female, as many have been used by their so called boyfriend and dumped.

CHAPTER THREE

- It is a sin to have sex when you are not legally married.
- It deadens your relationship with God, because of the guilt of sexual sin which runs through your conscience any time you are in God's presence.
- Cohabiting couples quarrel often, even when they eventually become legally joined as husband and wife, because the marriage often happens only because the woman became pregnant, so the man sees it as a forced marriage.
- There is a tendency for both to continue cheating by seeing other sex partners. This may pose a serious health challenge to both of them as the chances of been infected with a venereal disease is high.
- Many single parents today are the result of cohabitation. This has led to many children becoming wayward in society.
- Economically, it is not wise to spend on a spouse who means little or nothing to your overall life plan.
- Drug addictions is increasing as a result of heart-breaking experiences in cohabiting.

CHAPTER FOUR

THE DOWRY

The dowry is more significant as a vow than for the material goods involved. Chambers Dictionary defines dowry as 'the property which a woman brings to her husband at marriage.' It also explains that it involves the gifts given to the woman on marriage and includes her endowment. This means that whatever training and upbringing or talents she has to bring into the marriage qualify as part of her dowry.

This varies from tribe to tribe. In some cases, when a suitor comes to ask for the hand of a lady in marriage, the parent, in accordance with the custom and tradition of the people, would ask the suitor to pay money as a price for his bride. In other cultures the bridegroom is asked to pay an amount of money which he feels represents the value he attaches to the bride. Though these are not fixed amounts, they are usually spent in buying gifts and household items for the woman as her dowry.

Some wealthy parents even go so far as to provide a

CHAPTER FOUR

mansion and a car, or even a business, for their daughter as a farewell gift, as part of the bride's wealth. I have seen situations where a whole expanse of land was given, which in some cases has been contested in the law courts.

After the offspring of the marriage union have grown they may try to claim a portion of the land back, with the excuse that it was given to the bride as a gift from their father, and as such does not belong to the community where the bride had gone to marry. In modern societies in the 21st century, marriages have grown out of the traditional setting into more of a contractual agreement. I am concentrating on what was practised by the chosen children of God, which to me must have been an ordained process accepted by God. Abraham would be a perfect example. He provided gifts for his servant to get Isaac a wife, and Rebecca's family also provided gifts for her to bring to her husband's home as they bade her farewell.

Jacob had no gift in his hand, but he served his in-law. Moses helped Zipporah to feed the father's flock and that was enough to earn him a wife. Every man desiring a wife should endeavour to seek the hand of the bride from her parents or guardian.

Spiritual aspect of the dowry
From what we have discussed above, we should look at the spiritual aspect of a dowry. Note that God took a rib from Adam in order to provide him a wife. The rib God took was

incorporated into what became Eve - whatsoever image she had at the presentation ceremony. This implies that the dowry should be enough to make the woman look presentable in accordance with the desire of the bridegroom.

When God presented Eve to Adam, it was Adam's approval that made God ordain marriage. If Adam had seen Eve as one of the beasts that God usually presented to him, that would have been the end of marriage. His approval shows that Eve was not an animal but someone comparable to him. This can be seen by his proclamation 'bone of my bone and flesh of my flesh'. This is why I am against brides dressing, eating and otherwise behaving like animals.

First God had to be able to stand with Eve, holding her hand and waiting for Adam to approve. Can many so-called brides stand in God's presence, not to talk of God holding their hand? Remember, our God is Holy and perfect. A Holy and perfect God would only hold the hand of a holy and perfect bride, and further present and recommend her before the groom who should have similar qualities too. Does this paint a picture in your mind of who a bride and her groom should be? This is the original spiritual order. Hence in Proverbs 18:22 we would see that God's approval of the marriage is the only way the marriage will experience the favour and glory of God. On wedding day, the bride's father is the one who would present his daughter to the man. Can

CHAPTER FOUR

fathers sincerely claim that they are presenting a bride that would succeed in marriage? Many of us pretend to the extent that we would lie before God, even as the minister echoes that whoever knows that the marriage should not be constituted should speak out. If our marriages are heading for the rocks, we should ask ourselves if God's favour is there.

From this discussion we may infer that the dowry must be approved by God for it to become an acceptable endowment for the woman to present. This takes us to the importance of training the bride to be filled with God's wisdom and the fear of the Lord, so that she can be led by God to her husband, because the Lord orders the footsteps of the righteous.

Adam named his wife, showing that the person who the bride becomes is named in the tongue of the man. The name a bridegroom calls his wife is an element of the dowry, judging from the dictionary definition of dowry. It was Eve's nature at that presentation ceremony that defined what the rib was formed into, and then what it represented: 'she shall be called Woman, because she was taken out of man', Genesis 2:23b.

Look at the last statement there: the dowry was the reason for the name she earned. And we would see Adam naming her again as Eve, in Genesis 3:20, because she would be the mother of all those living. This is as a result of the endowment she saw in her: her natural beauty (not because she enhanced

CHAPTER FOUR

her body with drugs or surgical operations), her breasts, her back shape (for carrying her child), etc. These assets were what she came into marriage with, as given to her by God. Her endowment to bear children gave her the name Eve. Today many men call their wives honey, dear, sweetheart, love, treasure etc, and the women will reply in like manner. A woman can see her dowry from the appreciation her husband shows to her daily. This is often shown to the children she bears also.

The dowry, in superlative terms, is a representation of culture and tradition. In this aspect, we would say it has a spiritual undertone that speaks of the kind of spiritual affiliation the bride may have been involved in as she was raised by her parents. And going by the fact that a dowry is a bride's endowment, we would say that marks on her body that dedicate her to gods and goddesses, tattoos which represent her soul being tied to the devil, her attitudes and characters, her beliefs, etc, will have a lot of influence on how the marriage finally survives.

God warned that the children of Israel should have nothing to do with the Canaanite daughters. This is because the Canaanite brides had been raised in idolatry and would therefore come into marriage with a dowry of idolatry.

This discussion demands that before a marriage is set in

CHAPTER FOUR

place, a holistic view should be addressed of who the individuals are spiritually, and they must give their lives to Christ if they have not done so already, otherwise the marriage will end up in the devil's net.

CHAPTER FIVE

THE SPIRITUAL IMPLICATIONS OF MARRIAGE

References to marriage and its significance to the relationship between God and His children is seen in the Old Testament, Isaiah 54:5, Jeremiah 3:14, Hosea 2:19 and in the New Testament, where the bridegroom is seen as Christ (Matthew 9:15, John 3:29) and the bride as His Church (2 Corinthians 11:2, Revelation 19:7, 21:2, 9).

The book of Malachi 2:12-16 implies that God values marriage. Here God says that a man who breaks faith with his wife will not be heard when he cries. God is a spirit, and since His interest is seen in marriage, it likewise shows that marriage is more of a spiritual affair than physical.

The intention of God in marriage was to create a one-man, one-woman relationship. This he achieved with the first marriage which He initiated and witnessed. The ordination of the marriage institute by God shows that we need to revere this institution with all spiritual obligations. Man, however, mutilated this institution. According to the Mosaic law,

CHAPTER FIVE

marriage was seen as a path to purity of life, so that one does not fall into sexual sins and immorality.

Going through the Bible, one would see that in the patriarchal age polygamy prevailed, Genesis 16:4, 25:1, 25:8, 28:9, 29:23, 26 and 1 Chronicles 7:14. This means that man's insatiability made him desire more wives, though polygamy was discouraged by Moses.

Divorce was also accepted as a means to settle marriage disagreements in the patriarchal age. An instance of this was recorded in Genesis 21:14. The Mosaic law also restricted divorce.

The Mosaic law sees marriage from a spiritual perspective and the various laws then attracted strict penalties and were seen as the best civil laws possible at the time, with the overall objective of bringing the people up to a pure standard of morality.

After the Jews returned from Babylonian captivity and the laws were read to them (Nehemiah 8:2-3) and explained by the Levites (Nehemiah 8:8), monogamy seemingly became the approved and more prevalent form of marriage. King Solomon had a thousand women, as wives and concubines, and also followed them to serve their idols. It was also recorded that Herod the Great had up to nine wives. Jesus mentioned to the men that it was their wickedness that made Moses allow them to divorce, as the abuse of divorce among them continued unabated.

CHAPTER FIVE

Our Lord in His teachings re-established the integrity and sanctity of the marriage union with the following principles:

- That marriage is the foundation of the church of Christ on Earth, by the confirmation of the original intention of God towards the institution, as an embryonic setting which develops into a virile, God-fearing society (Matthew 19:4, 5).

- That divorce is restricted to the case of fornication, and the prohibition of the remarrying of all divorcees and divorcers, if such was done without the proof of fornication, once any of the parties are still alive (Matthew 5:32, 19:9, Romans 7:3, 1 Corinthians 7:10-11). This however has led in crime-infested societies to men and women murdering their spouses so that they are free from their marriage bond and can remarry. In other cases, many have decided to separate while still claiming to be married. This is often listed on forms as 'separation,' where you also see itemized boxes where one would tick either 'married' or 'single.'

The New Testament, Hebrew 13:4, for instance, enforces moral purity in marriage and the formal condemnation of fornication (Acts 15:20).

Significance of marital vows
Vows are known to bind the soul, as implied in the book of Numbers 30:2. Marriage itself consists of vows and binds the two people together (Ephesians 5:31). Since the allegorical

CHAPTER FIVE

and typical references to marriage have an exclusive relationship to how it exhibits the spiritual relationship between God and his people, we would at this juncture discuss the main element of the marriage process, which is the performance of the marriage vow. A vow is defined as a solemn promise made to God to perform or to abstain from performing a certain thing. The Bible mentioned how Jacob vowed unto God (Genesis 28:18-22, 31:13), showing that the making of vows has existed for ages.

Another instance of the mention of vows is in the book of Job 22:27. The book of Psalms 76:11 explicitly says that we should make vows unto God and pay them. Marriage vows are made in the presence of God, right in His altar before the congregation and witnesses present, which puts a demand on the couple to fulfil. Below is an extract which I wrote for a typical marriage session which I have also officiated, and we would see the vow embedded:

Greetings from the minister:

I greet you all here present because of the union in marriage of Juliet and John. May the Lord bless you and grant you peace of eternal life in Jesus name.

ALL: Amen.

The rites of marriage:

Juliet and John, you appear before the altar of the Lord this day as man and wife, recognised by the law of the federal

CHAPTER FIVE

republic of Nigeria, to render your heart in service to God your creator, who fashioned you after His image and likeness. You are here this day to enter into a covenant with God in the presence of the congregation here present, whom you have invited to witness your confession before the Lord this day, to obey the command of the Lord in Genesis 2:24; Therefore shall a man leave his father and his mother, and shall cleave unto his wife: and they shall be one flesh. Marriage is a symbolic representation of the relationship between God and His children as seen in Jeremiah 31:32. The union called marriage is more of a spiritual affair and that is why Satan is in the business of breaking marriages. It has to do with the bonding together of two separate lives that have existed independently.

God instituted marriage so that one can complement the other; that the husband can sustain the wife and vice versa, physically, emotionally and spiritually. Marriage is God's ordained institution for raising up generations that fear God and do His will. In trying to dishonour this purpose, the world went into human cloning all in the name of science, but God has always proved them wrong. We should take heed therefore that we are not deceived by the world but to honour the command of the Lord to marry.

So it shall be that Juliet and John shall fulfil the purpose of marriage before God this day in Jesus' name.

CHAPTER FIVE

ALL: Amen

Exchange of vows:

Minister: John, your marriage to Juliet is recognized by the law of the federal republic of Nigeria, are you willing to honour the word of God in Ecclesiastes 9:9, which says 'Live joyfully with the wife whom you love all the days of your vain life which He has given you under the sun, all your days of vanity; for that is your portion in life, and in the labour which you perform under the sun'?

John: Yes I do.

Minister: Juliet, your marriage to John is recognized by the law of the federal republic of Nigeria, are you willing to honour the word of God and to be a virtuous woman all the days of your life, and that you will do your husband good and not evil all the days of your life as written in Proverbs 31:12?

Juliet: Yes I do.

Blessing of ring

Minister: Lord, I bless these rings, which are a token of the oath they perform before you this day. I pray that these rings will mark the beginning of your favour upon their lives in the name of the Father, of the Son and of the Holy Spirit.

ALL: Amen.

John: Juliet, with this ring I John wed you. It is a token of the love I profess to you, that nothing shall make me stop loving you all the days of my life and to abide in the oath of

CHAPTER FIVE

marriage we enter together in the presence of God this day, till death do us part.

Juliet: John, I give you this ring as a symbol of my love and faithfulness. As I place it on your finger, I commit my heart and soul to you. I ask you to wear this ring as a reminder of the vows we have spoken today in the presence of God, till death do us part.

Minister: John, you may now kiss your wife.

Congregation claps as they kiss

Congregational Blessing:

The congregation prays for the couple, asking God to grant them the fruit of the womb, provide for them financially, protect them from the affliction of the evil one and strengthen them to carry on with the task of marriage ahead of them and to give them the wisdom to raise up their children in the fear of God.

Minister's blessing:

Minister prays for them and anoints the couple.

Presentation of couples:

Minister: I present to you the latest and most favoured couple in town.

ALL: A hand of applause as the couple go back to sit together.

The Law of Moses did not introduce vow making but regulated the practice of vows, and these sets of vows would

CHAPTER FIVE

also help to establish the elemental terms in a marital vow. They include, but are not limited to:

Vow of devotion

This has to do with the service of the Lord. During the marriage process, including the marriage class, it is often reiterated that the reason for marriage is to revere God, who instructed that marriage should be constituted between a man and a woman.

Vow of submission

This includes faithfulness and dedication on the part of both the man and the woman to the purpose of the marriage covenant they have entered into. They are to encourage each other as they bear the burden of raising a generation of children that will serve God. The Bible says in Ephesians 2:21 that they should submit to each other in the fear of the Lord. A man who fears God will honour his wife, likewise a woman who fears God will honour her husband.

Vow of the headship of the man

God says that Abraham will command his family after Him. This establishes the man's authority and headship over the affairs of his home. On the day of the marriage, the bridegroom, taking the lead, shows that he is making a vow to ensure he does this all the days of his life.

Vow of abstinence

The vow of abstinence in marriage is like a two-edged

sword. One side has to do with the couple abstaining from sex during a period of spiritual reawakening involving fasting and prayer, which is a requirement to strengthen their marriage as they seek the face of God together. This is the whole essence of dedicating their marriage to God on that day of their wedding. The other side of the sword is the couple vowing to forgo every other relationship they were in prior to their marriage. Any breach of this would mean the sin of adultery, and we are told that no adulterer or adulteress will make heaven. If a couple can spend time with God, they will be able to spend time together, and at the end of the day, their marriage will be fenced away from unhealthy interaction with the world. This means that in the vow of abstinence, dedication to God is important to fulfilling the vow.

Vow of destruction

'Till death do us part' is a vow of destruction. This is based on the fact that all sins lead to death. Any act of unfaithfulness is sin and would naturally lead to a broken marriage. And since God is honoured when we keep vows, it would follow that when we are unfaithful, we are also heading for destruction.

Elements of marital vows

From the extract above, we would see the following as the substance of the marital vow: Biblical citations, the legal element in place as a proof of being tenable in a law court, ring, congregation present, kissing as a sign of unity, and the minister's proclamation, representing the involvement of God in the vow.

Punishment for breaking the marriage vow
The book of Malachi 2:16 indicates that the prayers of whoever breaks faith with the spouse will not be answered. Though this verse refers to man, it would also be extended to what would happen to a woman who broke faith with her husband.

Spiritual aspect of the marriage process
This is like fusing back the lost rib into the man, so to speak. Spiritually, it involves soul knitting. Since God presented the first woman to man, it shows us that marriage is not merely about sexual satisfaction, as has been propounded by many advocates of sex in marriage. The spiritual aspect of the marriage process revolves around the facts that:

1. Immediate or ancestral genealogical blessings are inherited from both.
2. Immediate or ancestral genealogical curses are inherited into the union from both.
3. Genes from both are seen in their offspring: the DNA from the child proves this.

4. Knowledge gained over the years by both will begin to shape the home, either positively or negatively. This means that there is no way both parties will remain who they used to be any more.
5. The fate of a whole nation is determined through this marriage.
6. Society will reap the fruits of the marriage, positive or negative: a king, queen, president, governor, pastor – many leadership traits will be developed in this home.
7. Biologically, hormonal transfer will also start to take place in both as they involve in sexual intercourse. Research has shown that the male hormone is identified when a blood sample is taken from a woman's genital area immediately after unprotected sex.
8. Diseases will be shared by both as they relate together in sex.
9. Both good and bad attitudes which already exist in both will become practised in the home.
10. Their physical appearance will also tend to show a resemblance, meaning that a new man and a woman have been formed.

Looking at all this, I am not comfortable that marriages should be allowed to take place when we are sure that the marriage that is about to be constituted will cause pain to God and society, and know that the parents-to-be don't have what it takes to raise a strong family.

CHAPTER SIX

WHY MARRIAGES BREAK UP

Marriage is made up of many parts, all geared towards creating a godly environment. Many married couples do not consider these aspects: emotional (joy, love, sex, child bearing), spiritual (godliness), social (relationship management), productivity (creativity, intelligence) and aesthetics (physical beauty, neatness, personal hygiene).

A wife is to be compared with her husband. You would not dream of building a skyscraper and marrying a woman who wants to live in a three-bedroom flat, for instance. So many men and women end up discovering that they are not meant for each other after years of trying to push along. Polygamy therefore is a result of disappointment, discouragement, emotional instability and spiritual emptiness.

While I was gathering information for this book, God somehow favoured me with already-made information. The first was what I saw in my home as I grew up with my parents and other marriage crises happened around our home.

CHAPTER SIX

Another source of information came from those whom I met daily who told me stories of marriage complaints and what many of them were going through. I also watched many movies, both locally made in Nigeria and from Hollywood, on the issue of single parents and failed marriages. So there was enough information to process to get this book together.

There was one case that really shocked me. A couple almost fought in my counselling office over the issue of his wife refusing to wear 'bum shorts' when they were driving in the car together, claiming that the shorts were what attracted him to her. Bum shorts in the bedroom are OK by me, but in the car, I don't encourage them, if you ask for my opinion!

I had to interview both men and women casually with a question and answer session. The beauty of this was that I never showed any seriousness about the information I was gathering so they couldn't have pretended in their responses. This has taken me about three years now since I started this book. Below are the results:

Question (men): Now that you know your spouse, would you have married her if you had known her this well?

The answers I got were dumbfounding. About 80% of the men said that they would not have married their wives if they had had the kind of knowledge they now had of her before they got married. This percentage was made up of those who claimed that their wives were liabilities, were not sexy/not

CHAPTER SIX

good in bed, prayed too much or were too spiritual, were troublesome, fashion crazy, couldn't cook a good meal, were dirty, had poor reasoning abilities, were not ready to be corrected, were lazy, controlled by their mother, controlled by their pastor, were too boring, talked too much, travelled with their boss wherever they went, were suspected of adultery, were selfish, watched too much TV, didn't like what the husband liked, demanded too much sex, were never satisfied, hated their relatives, travelled a lot, didn't like travelling, were too academic or dullards, not prudent, too worldly, visited all manners of prophets and witch doctors, had seduced them, had hooked them with pregnancy, had produced no child, had taken them from their friends, etc.

These answers gave me sleepless nights. The 20% who said they would stick with their wives gave me the most astonishing secret about why many men marry. These last men actually said they would marry a woman because she was not a liability to them. She was, in most cases, the breadwinner in the house. She brought in the money, cooked the meals, bought clothes, paid the children's school fees, bought the cars they drove, was their spiritual backbone, etc. They claimed she was an asset they would die for anytime, come rain or shine.

Among these 20% also were the poor, who concluded that they were not sure any other woman would have accepted

CHAPTER SIX

them because of who they were, especially now that many young ladies were going after money. This also negated their decision, which means they would have married another woman if they were not who they are.

I know you will be waiting to hear the women's side of the story.

Question (Women): Now that you know your spouse, would you have married him if you had known him this well?

As usual with women, they quickly said, 'Why not? He is my everything'. Then I would probe further and they would open up, saying 'My husband would be a good man if it weren't for outside influences – his mother, sisters, friends – especially the bad ones who don't have a wife yet. He doesn't listen to me, he hates paying his tithes, he doesn't pray with the family, he doesn't care for my relatives, even my parents, but he spends all the money on his relatives. We don't have quality sex and I suspect him of having a woman outside. I don't know his salary, he is too secretive. He drinks, he smokes, he doesn't like my food, he doesn't pay the children's school fees, he is being controlled by his mother, the family are idol worshippers, he deceived me that he was a Christian', etc. And they would conclude: 'what will I do? I am just in that marriage for the sake of my children, and because I know that God frowns at divorce'.

This percentage was about 93%. Even those I felt were

CHAPTER SIX

enjoying a quality marriage in terms of what money can buy confirmed otherwise. The 7% who said they would still have married their present husband also confirmed the fears they had: 'He was there for me when my parents were sick, without him I wouldn't have finished my schooling since I had no one to train me in school, he is the one sustaining my parents and siblings, he is a handsome and quiet gentle man, my husband, he is my jewel – a sex machine and a horse in bed, he met me when I was a virgin so I don't know what other men feel like, he is very caring, he loves me more that his relatives, I don't have a mother-in-law problem because she was dead before we married, he is the only son of his parents and has all the estates willed to him… Pastor I don't have a choice – I only married who God gave to me, my husband is God-sent – he never looks at any other woman, I married him because he is rich and ready to spend – in short he is Any Time Money (ATM)', etc.

As I put all these together in this book, I have also been wondering why marriages have turned out this way. The question now is how we can salvage our marriages from decay. This is because of the important role marriage plays in the growth of the church and in society development. Children from broken homes in most cases become hoodlums – armed robbers, kidnappers, rapists, prostitutes, God-haters, dullards, political thugs, poor leaders, etc.

CHAPTER SIX

The information above shows the reasons why many marriages are already heading to the rocks. It is somewhat difficult to explain why marriages break up, as it is not usually a one-day event. Break-ups happen gradually over the years until such a time when both of them start seeing each other as enemies with whom they cannot live. We are told in Psalms 11:3: *'When the foundations are being destroyed, what can the righteous do?'*

From this verse, we can conclude that any marriage that is not working is devoid of God's presence. And if we look at break-ups, we would see that both parties have disregarded the fact that a marriage is a sacrifice to bring up a new generation unto God. If we see this we would know how to make a choice of a marriage partner, and how to endure the odds that would come as we live together.

There is a cost attached to every sacrifice. Marriage is a sacrifice, and as such we should expect to pay a price to keep it refreshed. The same problem that is affecting Christianity today is also affecting marriage. Worldliness is eating deep into our marriages. We either demand more sex or more money. And these two elements have never regarded God.

Many married couples practise pornographic acts - if it is not oral sex, then it is anal sex. Even pregnancy is becoming a laboratory exercise. What did St Paul experience as he preached the word? Many of his converts were still glued to

CHAPTER SIX

their old adamic lives, and to make matters worse many of them were practising sodomy. The reasons behind our complaints in marriage are mainly centred on selfish, egotistic satisfaction, not because we want to revere God in our marriages.

If we saw marriage as a process that enhances the fulfilment of God's will on earth, we would live in joy. When I remember Jacob and his two wives, and how they hunted him around with sexual overtures in order to have more children (including offering their housemaids), I see the reason for marital failures. Both Leah and Rachael died before their husbands. There was no peace in the home. There was a difference between them (Genesis 29:17). This difference later played a major role in what happened in the home - Leah was hated and Rachael was loved by their husband. God had to intervene and give Leah children.

Polygamy is not good in the eyes of God, because it always gives Him the reason to take bitter decisions, loving one and hating the other, as it may seem wise in His eyes. We also see this in Abraham. Sarah and Haggai bred hatred in the home, and when Sarah died, we are told that Abraham had to settle his other children through Keturah in order that peace should reign.

Did God tell Abraham to sleep with Haggai and Keturah? Was it not because both Sarah and Abraham wanted who will inherit Abraham's wealth? Abraham had showed his fears before

CHAPTER SIX

God in making Eliezer his heir. Today we find it hard to live for God because we are afraid of who takes over our inheritance.

I read about Shakespeare, who does not have any lineage living today. Is he unpopular today? No! He still lives on. Marriage to me is therefore a pool of couples, joined together in common faith for the purpose of establishing the kingdom of God on earth. Anything devoid of this will breed hatred and breakup, because it is resting on a foundation which was not formed on godly intentions.

We would at this point treat the various parts of marriage that were mentioned earlier:

1. Emotionally dead marriage
An emotionally dead marriage is one where there is no togetherness created by warm feelings of care for each other's need. Emotion breeds joy, love, care and sexual activeness. The offshoot of all these is the ability to endure one another and to forgive one another in the family. The lack of child bearing also destabilises the emotional balance in the home in some cases, especially when both the husband and the wife start being attacked from outside. In other cases, the absence of one child sex in the home also breeds discomfiting compromises, as either of them may end up carrying out acts that will jeopardize the marriage vow they entered into in God's presence.

CHAPTER SIX

An emotionally dead marriage is devoid of God's presence, because the Godhead is an emotional being. Jesus had compassion on those He finally healed, because of their perseverance in sustaining the life they had and their vehement desires to come out of their ugly situation. A home that is dead emotionally grows thorns and thistles, and as such there is no premises for godliness to strive. The result will be a broken home.

2. Spiritually dead marriage

Closely related to what we discussed above is spiritual deadness. God informed Adam that the day they ate of a tree in the middle of the garden, they would die. They did indeed die after their sin, which was displayed in the shame they experienced. Why should they be ashamed when it was only the two of them who were in the garden?

A spiritually dead marriage lives in shame because both have become devoid of the wisdom of God. The book of Jeremiah 8:9 says that the wise men have become ashamed because they have neglected the wisdom of the Lord. Any married couple who have dishonoured God should not expect peace, because God is the 'author and finisher' of our peace, because faith is the foundation of peace. Without Him in us, there is no peace in our lives.

The fear of God in any home is the beginning of the

wisdom that will help sustain that home. I would advise that on no account must any member of the family spend a day outside the wisdom of God. The man should take charge in bringing his family before God, and training them on what to do to imbibe the favour and wellbeing nature of God. This way, the marriage will smell sweet unto God as a holy sacrifice before Him.

Many women have decided to avoid their husbands because they belong to an occult organization or are not serious with God. While I will not support this act, I have equally come to realize what the Bible says about walking together (Amos 3:3). This is why I always say that every man or woman must wait on God before they can marry.

3. Socially dead marriage
This has to do with relationship management. How do we interact with each other? How do we also relate with outsiders? Some people have blamed their break-up on the fact that either the man or the woman could not socialize, finding it difficult to welcome friends into the home, while others have complained that their partner was too sociable, welcoming every Tom, Dick and Harry. There is no hard truth about this, but I would advise that even as we have introverts and extroverts, each of them should know their limits in socialising.

I am quite sure that the children of Israel were sociable

people. Miriam was able to approach Pharaoh's daughter, Moses, even as a stranger, would help to draw water for people he hadn't seen before. Jesus displayed this social attribute when He dined and wined with the low and high classes. The Israelites had lots of ceremonial feasts, which were acts of sociability. The feast of Purim in the days of Esther was a sociable event.

Any unsociable person should not marry, because marriage is about communication. A socially-dead marriage is one in which there is no effective communication in the home. Communicate your fears in time, before it is taken over by events that will lead to dissociation.

4. Productively dead marriage
I love creativity, resourcefulness and intelligence. I find it hard to get on with dull people. This seems to be a problem in me which I am trying to work on. I expect that before I ask a question, the answer should be known by everyone present. This implies that someone married to me might occasionally get frustrated with my level of demands. I don't expect people to make the same mistake over and over again. I easily get pissed off with such people. My drive is for excellence.

This characteristic of mine almost broke my marriage. My wife studied mass communication, while I am an engineer. My training over the years, including my background from

CHAPTER SIX

my home, saw me as one who is not comfortable with 'Near-Success Syndrome.' She didn't have the kind of training I have gone through, though she could easily give the kind of advice that will put things in order. She was seemingly finding it difficult with my jet-paced answers and demands. She would occasionally snap back at me and I will back off, to come back later.

Our home was growing colder by the day, as we hardly talked. To make matters worse I developed an interest in writing, while she was glued to her TV programmes and movies. We had separate lives for about two years. Everywhere around us was cold, and she would occasionally tell me she would prefer us to go our separate ways.

Then, when the ministry started after I had answered the call of God, she suddenly became very productive, supporting me here and there, and she became the perfect wife I had wanted.

Why did I recount this story? The facts are clearly spelt out. There is nobody who is not productive. It may just be that his/her talent is not matching what is needed there and then. The moment there is a shift in vocation, productive excellence may spring forth. I have heard men say that their wives are 'liabilities,' simply because they are not gainfully employed. I don't think so. Bringing up children is a job no one can pay for. A woman who runs the home is as valuable

CHAPTER SIX

to me as a professionally-employed woman who has to employ the services of a nanny, cleaner and cook to help her fulfil her obligation to her husband.

In these homes also, the men have also complained of not being served food by their wives. We should set out the facts that will sustain our homes and stop us quarrelling. A young man once lost his wife to adultery because he was comparing her with other women who were gainfully employed in the oil and gas industry. She started by having late-night chats with young men on Yahoo Messenger and Skype. She started practising phone sex, and then real sex.

While it is good for a woman to engage herself in a trade, there is no guarantee that she will bring money in to help sustain the home because she will over time develop her own needs, which may not help the vision of the home.

I have also seen that those whom people think are having a blissful marriage, because of the wealth they see around them, often have no peace in their homes. No two homes can be exactly the same. We all have our peculiarities. My candid advice is that we should seek God's wisdom in whatever we do and we will become productive and creatively intelligent in managing our homes.

5. Aesthetically dead marriage
Necessity is the mother of invention. This is where novelty comes in. Closely related to the social aspect of human life is

CHAPTER SIX

aesthetic beauty. We were created to appreciate beauty. This includes physical beauty, neatness, personal hygiene, etc. Many of us have travelled to beautiful cities and places to have a sight of the beauty man has created. Everything that exists on earth is created in various shapes and sizes. This is the intent of God's pulse that beats in us.

When either the man or woman becomes dirty and smells obnoxiously, there is every chance that the marriage is heading towards termination. We should look at the flowers in the garden, and see how we can create a lovely home for ourselves. We should employ the use of fragrance to keep the home wonderful. The breeding of germs in our homes will give room to illnesses and then we will be spending much on health.

Prostitutes entice their prey with beauty. Every woman should learn to live in beauty. On the wedding day every woman looks her best, and even the dirtiest man will have his hair cut and his armpits cleaned up. Why then do we live in filth after the wedding? Whom are we deceiving? Sooner rather than later our acts of dirtiness will be spread in public when we quarrel, and passers-by will find out that our dirtiness is the reason behind the quarrel. What a shame!

CHAPTER SEVEN

SUSTAINING THE MARRIAGE

Many marriages are suffering from family habits that have developed over the years. Some are spiritual and others are physical. Many marriages fail as earlier discussed, because the reason behind the initial constitution of the marriage bond was not to honour God. Once this reason no longer exists, or other factors have rendered it passive, the marriage will begin to suffer the coldness of death.

In the section that follows we shall be addressing these factors, and these will be seen in who the man and the woman actually choose.

Men want a wife who represents various aspects of their lives as the years grows by. In the section that follows we will discuss these aspects of a man's life and how he wants his wife to fit into every sphere of his life. This is where a wife's role as a companion comes into play, and becomes so pronounced that without her presence, the man is incomplete.

CHAPTER SEVEN

Early years

Between the ages of 25 to 30 the young man is full of life and may be trying to grow out of juvenile delinquency. He is growing into adulthood, wants to be in charge of his life and does not want anyone interfering with his decisions. He feels on top of the world, and would want to be respected and noticed wherever he is.

Many who are believers are more energetic at this age. Sexual desire is experienced almost every day. This is because many feel they have been deprived of the act for too long. They have many friends – including female admirers who were unfortunate in not being allowed their favoured marriage partner. Their sense of appreciation of beauty is greater, as may be seen in the cars they prefer to drive and the way they want their homes to be decorated. Though things may not be so fascinating around them, they love to be appreciated as having achieved what they have.

A woman marrying a man at this age is likely to be in the same age bracket and can cope with the type of life he lives. This is why she must work on her beauty, home-keeping, respect and adoration, and maintain a good spiritual sense to be able to sustain the marriage. The man is learning to be a man, and the woman is learning to be a wife.

Sexual drive is on the increase, and sooner rather than later children will arrive, giving the wife more responsibilities,

CHAPTER SEVEN

which the man may not have been planning for. He is still wasting money on objects of fashion and state-of-the-art electronic gadgets. He doesn't want his friends, especially the unmarried ones, to see him as dropping out. He wants to be with them watching football, and is often seen making worthless phone calls, all in the name of not being seen to be fading out of relevance. He is still close to the parents with whom he celebrated his graduation, so the wife may still notice a high level of interference from his relations.

The key is that the wife must show him enough love and sexual presence. A good wife would encourage him to be steadfast with the Lord. Many marriages break at this stage, because the man feels he is still of very high value. The wife wants to keep the marriage, but the husband is still contemplating if he is ready to continue being controlled by his wife. There is lots of friction here over who does what.

Early middle age
This is between the ages of 31 to 35. The man is getting used to his wife and they have learned from their mistakes. They are also trying to maintain each other's respect, so many things have been let go. The man's ego is under better control and he may no longer be pushing his weight as the breadwinner of the house. There may be children now, and he has to plan with his wife to pay school fees. He is also

involved now in more responsible duties in his workplace, and getting more involved in leadership-related roles. So he is becoming more of a leader than a boss at home, and he may not be too sex crazy anymore because he has more responsibilities now in his hands.

This is where many wives fight their husbands because they suddenly discover that they don't seem to go after them for sex the way they used to. He needs a planner as a wife at this stage. He may not take so much interest in his wife's hairstyle. Some will keep long beards and may look unkempt. This is where the knowledgeable wife ought to keep the home enticing and romantic, though she also has a lot to do with caring for the children. She may also be facing in-laws' challenges as they no longer see so much of their son and brother, who has so much on his mind. Some young men obviously start to think about what will become of their marriage after the age of 60 years.

Middle Age

I see this age bracket as between the ages of 35 to 40. The man is regaining the trust of his wife. There have being some quarrels over his behaviour, and he is seeking counselling from the elderly in order to cope with what he now sees. He wants peace in his home.

CHAPTER SEVEN

He may suddenly start demanding sex, and any act of refusal from his wife will make him angry. He wants to feel young, shaving his beard again. He is more engrossed in roles of leadership now. He wants to take the lead and encouraging other young people around him.

The wife in most cases has become cold to sex due to the experience she had with his diminishing sexual drive in the last phase. Quarrels happen as she continuously refuses him, because she had earlier occupied her mind with other thoughts. Some would become more business conscious, and work harder in the office, and want to derive joy outside sex and their home.

Many are seen wanting counselling. The man complains of the wife's negligence of her marital obligation more often. The children wake up at night to see mum and dad quarrelling. They won't give the reason for the quarrel, but it is all about sex and money. The wife uses demands for money for the family upkeep to push the man off, while the man uses the demand for sex to push her off her financial demands.

The quarrelling at this stage prepares the couple for the maturity phase, where they now work to build their home on a solid rock that will see them through the remaining part of their lives. Any marriage that can succeed to this stage will definitely make it through.

CHAPTER SEVEN

Late middle age

This, between 41-50 years, is the age of acceptance. The man wants to be accepted, no matter what. For those who are workers in God's vineyard, he is becoming more of a teacher and mentor, and would use his experience to start counselling others. He wants to be believed and would want others to see him as someone who has garnered much experience over the years. He often wants to mention his wife as his witness in all that he is saying. And the wife is also proud to be there as they recount their experiences.

If they have had children early, they may be at university, and the in-laws will have gone to take care of their own homes, so the woman is getting less interference from outside. This is the period when the man also gets more involved in capital projects and money may become scarce, though many may have invested more before this time. It all depends on what the couple see as priority in their life. Her trust in her husband's heart increases. She wants her husband to desire her for sex. She wants to be cared for and shown real affection. Many women also complain that their husband is not giving attention to them and may dress to attract his attention as if they are young girls. This is understandable - she fears the menopause. She is afraid her husband may be seeing a younger woman. Some still nag their husbands at this stage.

CHAPTER SEVEN

Perennial age

I see this as age 50 and above, when there seems to be no more discovery. The man is gradually planning for retirement. He is engrossed with the future of his children, and how to see they do not become a burden to him. He has grown now in the service of God, and in other leadership roles. His calm and mature nature may not go well with his wife except that both of them are almost within the same age group. Many women who are married to this age group of men suspect their husbands of infidelity, because they become less interested in sex, though many take drugs to become sexually active. The quarrels you notice in this home have much to do with sex.

In all age bands we have discussed, couples can sustain their marriages through:

- Raising a family altar for family fellowship and reverence of God in the home. This helps to focus everyone on the promises of God.
- Conducting fasting and prayers for the sustenance of the marriage and the future of the children.
- Imbibing the spirit of tolerance and forgiveness.
- Planning for the future together – children, finance, savings, contentment level, etc.
- Mutual respect for each other's opinion.
- Involvement in acts of godliness to others – welfare service.

CHAPTER SEVEN

- Attending church services together.
- Making vows of commitment for each other and to God.
- Celebrating their wedding anniversary every year.
- Attending marriage seminars together.
- Get employed (self–develop your God-given talent)
- Paying tithes together
- Praying for other marriages, to help them too to see the faults in their homes.

CHAPTER EIGHT

THE CASE FOR MEN

There is a special verse of the Bible that caught my attention some time in 2005, and ever since then I have lived by it. This verse says: *Live joyfully with the wife whom you love all the days of the life of your vanity, which he has given you under the sun, all the days of your vanity: for that is your portion in this life, and in your labour which you take under the sun* - Ecclesiastes 9:9

If many men understood what their own 'portion' is in this world of turmoil, they would live to cherish and secure it. When we buy properties that mean much to us, we secure them with all the legal requirements that are needed because we don't want to lose them.

Today many marriages are in a shambles because God is absent in the home. Every family is supposed to be a mini-worship centre or church where God's presence is always felt, and the creation of this kind of a home is the husband's responsibility. Many men drink alcohol with their wives and in most cases the women yield to the man's way of life so as not to lose him to the women of his kind.

CHAPTER EIGHT

Most men will easily conclude that their wives are bad or evil. She may be evil, but certainly most of the evil tendencies in her life were made manifest as a result of your interactions with her, because if you had known she was evil in the first place, you wouldn't have married her.

Men often invent pet names to call their new found love, and some will say she is a godsend. But by marriage, she may become 'sent by the devil'. If the Bible, as recorded in Ecclesiastes 9:9, told us that the wife is the husband's only treasure and reward in this earth, then every wife needs to be treated with passion, care and adoration.

God gave every man a wife so as to protect him from the cold hand of the grief of loneliness. For any man to treat that gift with levity, disdain, disrespect and disregard is evil before God, and any man who maltreats his wife is out of tune with God. Such a man does not have a place in God's kingdom. He is a wolf in sheep's clothing and does not deserve to live.

The woman is the emblem of perfection created out of creation, and this is why she will find any means to put the home in order by complaining to anyone who she thinks can offer a solution to the trouble in her home, because women cannot exist alone. They are a creation from a creation and therefore derive their day-to-day strength from the source creation (in this case their husband). This is why the Bible let us know that the woman is the glory of the man (1 Corinthians 11:7).

CHAPTER EIGHT

When a man makes his wife seek assistance from outside the home to make the marriage work, the woman is found to have solace outside, in most cases, in the hands of witch doctors. Because the man's foolishness is the reason behind the woman's sorrow, the man receives greater condemnation. The Bible said in Matthew 18:7 'woe to that person who is behind the temptation'.

Why a man must make his marriage work
The following reasons will enable every man to know that they have a responsibility to make their marriage work.

1. No going back after professing love
Every man has said 'I love you' to his wife at one time or another. The phrase is a vow and an oath before the woman and God, the secret witness. When a man now turns back to hate or expose the woman's nakedness in shame to the outside world, he has broken the oath and the vow, and such a man will surely be held responsible for whatever results from that act.

To love means to release and yield the substance of strength in you to the recipient (in this case the wife). When God gave the world His only son (John 3:16), He yielded his strength to the world because in the book of John 1:3, the Bible told us that Jesus Christ is the reason behind every creation of God. The love of God is the reason we are alive

CHAPTER EIGHT

today. How can a man therefore strangle life out of his wife by maltreating her and allowing her to die in sorrow and uncared for?

2. A wife is man's licence to obtain God's favour

Every man should understand that a wife is a 'Favour Bearer.' She is the medium through which a man can obtain God's favour (Proverbs 18:22), and I will quickly tell you what favour entails; God's favour upon any man is an uncensored and unconditioned release of blessings from Almighty God. This is why the saying goes 'behind any successful man, there is a wise woman'.

God denies every man who maltreats his wife this, God's given favour. This is why you see such men struggling with everything in their lives - they feel isolated, dejected and unwelcome wherever they are. Everything around them is dead and they yield to drunkenness, smoking, sexual maladjustment, demonic stone heartedness, satanic manoeuvres, unhealthy parental interference (especially from their mothers and sisters), etc. The good men in society often avoid them because they stink spiritually and lack remorse for the evil they commit.

I can sense God talking to somebody this day – hey, don't be stone hearted. God wants you to have a successful earthly living because he is surely going to judge every man. The avenue for change is before you. If you are a man breaking faith with your wife, use it now and correct the wrongs in your home.

3. The man is the head of the family

The Bible told us that the man is the head of the family, and when the head is corrupt what becomes of the body? 1 Timothy 5:8 made it clear that every man who cannot provide for his own family is worse than an infidel. There is no man who will tell me he provides adequate clothing, food and shelter for the woman he calls evil. Even at that, provision is not about this, it circumscribes such emotional integrations including love, care and the like. The love a man has for his children is normally an extension of that which he has for his wife, and when a man hates his wife, in likewise manner, he extends the hatred to his children.

Making your marriage work

In Genesis 6:9 the Bible let us know that because Noah found favour with God, he was rescued from destruction – he and his entire household. There is no other way to make our marriage work than to yield to God and repent from the sin resulting from the pollution in our heart as recorded in the book of Mark 7: 21-23:

For from within, out of the heart of men, proceed evil thoughts, adulteries, fornications, murders, Thefts, covetousness, wickedness,

CHAPTER EIGHT

deceit, lasciviousness, an evil eye, blasphemy, pride, foolishness: All these evil things come from within, and defile the man.

When a man finds favour with God, he will be rescued from destruction, including marital trouble, which is destruction aimed at every marriage from the pit of hell and must be resisted. We are informed that whatever we bind on Earth is forever bound in heaven (Matthew 18:18). So keep every marital trouble in your marriage bound as from today.

If you want peace in your marriage, every man should resist the following:

1. Not worshipping in the same church as your wife. Both of you must worship together in a living church and also study the Bible and pray together. A family that prays together thrives together.
2. Unfounded suspicion of your wife's sexual misconduct outside marriage.
3. Interference from your mother and sisters.
4. Having extra-marital affairs.
5. Bad habits, including drinking, smoking, keeping late nights and non-Christian friends.
6. Absence from church or godly gatherings. You will end up raising up children who will turn out to become devourers of you and society.

CHAPTER EIGHT

7. Keeping close contact with unmarried women, even when you feel no string is attached, because some day you may see the other side and become desperate to attach a string that will devour you.

8. Hiding secrets from your wife. If you know you cannot open your heart to your wife, why did you marry her in the first place? If you see her as an alien, then she cannot be your wife. She is supposed to be bone of your bone and flesh of your flesh (Gen. 2:23).

Every man should encourage the following:

1. Constant communication: Always talk openly; every word you speak shows what you harbour in your heart (Matthew 12:34).

2. Frequent body contact and passion display (1 Corinthians 7:3-5)

3. Separate yourselves from the troubles of the world and be together – just the two of you - and show her love. Sing some love songs to her - don't be out of tune! Study Songs of Solomon in the Bible and you will discover that you have not started loving your wife yet.

4. Family Bible study at home. If you discover a change in her attitude, let her take the lead in the Bible study session and ensure that the topic for discussion is the ungodly habit she is exhibiting. Topics can also be designed to

encourage her and to praise her motherly care in the home. In some cases these topics should be handled by those of your children who are old enough to lead the session.

5. Above all, pray that the Holy Spirit directs you on how to manage the home. This is because God is already managing the world and the Holy Spirit who is the agent of this management process has gotten lots of experience to share with the man. It is a man's responsibility to manage his home, which happens to be a microcosm of the larger macrocosm.

Reconciliation
If God is talking to you and you want a happy and blissful marriage, pray this prayer:

My Heavenly father, I know I have gone astray in my attitude and behaviour towards my wife and children. I am sorry for my actions. Please forgive me and give me the wisdom to make my marriage work. I promise to love and care for my family always. My wife is my heart and I will always cherish and love her. I appreciate her as a gift from you to better my life.

Thank you heavenly father, In Jesus Christ name I pray. Amen.

You have made all things right before God this day and you will see your family responding to these spoken words. Shalom!

CHAPTER NINE

THE CASE FOR WOMEN

Every woman desires to be a virtuous woman, because of the exemplary qualities that the Bible outlined about her. 'Who can find a virtuous woman? for her price is far above rubies' (Proverbs 31:10). And the Bible also says 'But a prudent wife is from God' (Proverbs 19:16).

Women are often too quick to start packing when there is a disagreement between them and their husbands, as if they were never prepared to raise a family unto God in the first place.

The characteristics of being qualified as a virtuous woman are difficult to attain, yet not unattainable. It is the totality of the being called 'woman' which Adam saw the very day God brought her to him. Every man is in search of this woman and even in the midst of 1000 women King Solomon could not find her (Ecclesiastes 7:28). And you don't have to kill yourself because you are lacking in one of those attributes of hers! With learning, understanding and adaptation, you will get there.

CHAPTER NINE

King Solomon said in Ecclesiastes 7:28 that out of a thousand women, he could not find one. Women abounded all around him daily, but God was able to find Mary. What are the men looking for in a woman that is making them search thus far? The search for her is what led Solomon to have a thousand women. So no woman should bother at this stage about whether she is a virtuous woman or not.

This is the same reason why the Bible told us that finding a woman is a requirement to getting a wife, and if out of a thousand there was no woman found, many men may have been living with a woman who is not a wife. The favour from God referred to in Proverbs 18:22 become manifest in the marriage when the woman became the crown to her husband (Proverbs 12:4), and as a crown the man becomes honoured and regarded above his colleagues (Proverbs 31:23). This is what makes people glorify God for her sake, because the good works of the woman in the house is manifested in her husband (Matthew 5:16).

If therefore in a thousand women, no woman could be found, then it means the attributes of a virtuous woman are not hereditary and therefore cannot be inherited from her mother. This leaves every woman with no other option but to undergo a gradual training process that will take them to the state of being virtuous or near-virtuous.

I would say that virtuousness in a woman is therefore born

CHAPTER NINE

out of a state of diligent observation, experimentation and adaptation to changes in characters and behaviours to factors surrounding her marriage as they occur. Such changes and subsequent adaptation should then be modelled according to the dominant observable behavioural reflexes explained in proverbs 31:10-31.

The attributes in Proverbs 31:10-31 are not exhaustive, especially given the demands of our present world, but Proverbs 31:26 made us understand that with wisdom, every woman can fulfil her duty in marriage. Every woman must enable her marriage to work by creating the necessary environment and opportunity to learn. This is self learning, and you have to avail yourself of the learning opportunities that come your way daily through quarrels, neglect by the man, hatred from his family and his friends etc. All of these have their roots. You must dig up that root, and to dig it up you need to be patient, observing and learning. These behaviours are certainly feedbacks, and they are essential in the learning and growing process. You are not alone. Every woman out there is undertaking this learning as you are doing. Do not be weary, you will soon get there.

Don't conclude that your husband is evil or mad. When you fail an examination, the teacher is not going to come smiling at you. He would rather put on a stern face to inform you all is not well and therefore you must sit up. While you are sitting up, the teacher will also go and research how better

CHAPTER NINE

to instil the learning in you, so that next time you will come out with flying colours.

God once destroyed the world with water (Genesis 6 & 7) and later sent his only begotten son to redeem the same world, even when the evil was now at its climax, more than in the days of Sodom and Gomorrah, because of the love He had for the world (John 3:16). The later solution proved to be better than the former and we are all enjoying it today. Your husband is the best man ever and he is also trying to figure out how best to make the marriage work.

Finding a good man is not easy either. The same Ecclesiastes 7:28 told us that out of a thousand men, only one suitable man was found. Your husband is also undergoing a learning process and all the defences he is putting on were occasioned by you, or from stories of other women he hears outside. Men gossip too - you know.

Why a woman must make her marriage work
Every woman has a duty before man and God to ensure that her marriage works. There are no excuses. The events surrounding her creation in Genesis 2:20b-24 answer it all:
...but for Adam there was not found an helpmeet for him.

21 And the LORD God caused a deep sleep to fall upon Adam, and he slept: and he took one of his ribs, and closed up the flesh instead thereof;

CHAPTER NINE

22 And the rib, which the LORD God had taken from man, made he a woman, and brought her unto the man.

23 And Adam said, This is now bone of my bones, and flesh of my flesh: she shall be called Woman, because she was taken out of Man.

24 Therefore shall a man leave his father and his mother, and shall cleave unto his wife: and they shall be one flesh.

A helpmeet must be there waiting until the master tells him/her to go and rest. The duty of building a blissful marriage relationship is a responsibility of both the man and the woman. Many women say: 'Well, he doesn't want to change, so what do you expect me to do?'

There is a lot they can do. The success of the supervisor depends on the extra work put in by the subordinate. Some women work, and I can confirm that none of them will see their bosses and stand discussing with friends when it is not lunchtime. Some women even go to the extent of pleasing their bosses by going to bed with them.

Making your marriage work is a serious affair, because that is where you are going to earn your honour and dignity (Proverbs 31:28), and remember, if you are not good in your home then you cannot be good outside – charity, they say, begins at home. This implies that since there is a reward waiting for you when your marriage works, you cannot wait to see your marriage rescued from destruction because:

CHAPTER NINE

1. The woman makes the home

A woman can either build her home or tear it down with her hands (Proverbs 14:1). Every woman should first ask herself the result of the actions they are about to carry out or the effect of their behaviour on the family. Let's look at a common example in our modern homes. If your child comes to tell you 'Mummy, I am hungry' and you call the house help to give the child food, you have lost that child to the house help. If you do this to your husband, then you just gave the man your handmaid to sleep with and she becomes a new wife for him. Many women will say 'the man is not ashamed, how can he descend so low to sleep with a dirty house girl?' Well you call her dirty - when you told her to serve your husband and children food, she was not dirty! Remember, 'What is good for the goose is good for the gander.' The cockerel always looks at the hand that brings the corn – so when you allow this to happen, the man will begin to discover the importance of the one you call the 'dirty house girl' and will put her to better use!

Some women come back late from work and cook late-night meals and expect the man to understand. I can tell you that you are gradually exposing him to temptation outside, because he will soon find comfort somewhere. In whichever way, whether a man chooses to become closer to God or closer to the outside world, he is no longer your man. He is either a

CHAPTER NINE

totally godly man who see no other thing but his Bible, or a total worldly man, who sees watching football, smoking, drinking, keeping late nights, cult membership, etc, as his comforter. Now even if he is a godly man and he studies his Bible and prays alone, you may be sure that you no longer have a husband. Such husbands, if care is not taken, easily backslide. Remember you are a part of him from creation and you need to be by him all the time - no excuses.

2. No going back after professing 'I love you'

As with the man, every woman has said 'I love you' to her husband on one occasion or the other. The phrase 'I love you' is a vow and an oath before the man and God who was the secret witness. This means that anything a woman does to undermine this declaration is an abomination before God.

To love a man means to yield and submit to him, or to be 'loyal to his government', so to say. Every man adores a submissive wife. Right from the days of creation as recorded in the book of Genesis 2:19, God gave man the authority of governance by relying on Adam to name all the animals you see today; in fact the Bible made it clear that God himself presented these animals to man - what a honour by Almighty God. If God relied so much on the wealth of judgment of the man He created, do not expect anything less from your man, because it will surely show in the home – and you cannot fight this.

CHAPTER NINE

This takes us to what the relationship between a woman's love for a man and her submissiveness to him entails. The relationship between God and the children of Israel, and by extension the world, was sometimes typified as a marriage relationship (Isaiah 54:5, Jeremiah 3:20, Jeremiah 31:32, Hosea 2:2, 7). God gave His only son to save the world (John 3:16), and the world in return must believe in the sacrifice He gave as a ransom for their sins to become saved.

Apart from believing in Jesus Christ, we must also yield and submit to the will of God as Christ did in Mathew 26:42 – wishing the cup should pass over him yet letting the will of God take pre-eminence. This is submission, and every woman should understand that they own the man and God a duty to perform their marital duties. The marital vows you make, the rings both of you wear, the togetherness you share on the undefiled bed, the sweet names you call yourselves etc, are enough evidence of the love you share.

I once defined love as 'Life of veritable evidence'. The veritability in the life both of you share together is your first point of exploration. Keep your eyes on his good behaviours, the behaviours you saw that makes you feel the man in him, the man you always desire. Now that your eyes are fixed on him as the best man in the world, let's drill down further.

CHAPTER NINE

Saving the marriage: the woman's place

As we get down to the main subject of discussion, 'Saving the Marriage', I will be talking about the fears of the woman, the battles she fights within her and her hopes. All these will be seen in the preceding teaching.

Mothers-in-law

This is the crux of the matter. Men respect their mothers so much and sometimes become attached to them to the extent that they are seen as 'mama's boys'. This is not supposed to be a problem, because most women are also attached to their fathers, but their own attachments begin to dwindle, because it was their father who handed them over to their husband on the wedding day. What nobody has asked is - who handed over the groom to the bride? His mother did, and because their own handover is not demonstrated, the attachment is still there and still strong.

In some cases, when the attachment becomes unwelcoming, it calls for a solution. This type of bonding is explained in Wikipedia below:

'Mother's boy, also called mama's boy, is a term for a man who is excessively attached to his mother at an age when men are expected to be independent (e.g. live on their own, be economically independent). A mother's boy may be effete or effeminate, or might be perceived as being macho, or might have a personality disorder,

CHAPTER NINE

such as avoidant personality disorder, or might be schizophrenic, so that the mother acts as a caretaker. In any case, a mother's boy cannot maintain a healthy partnership with a woman (Carruthers, 1998). Being mother-bonded is sometimes seen as a sign of weakness, and has a social stigma attached to it in many places, although in other places it may be more acceptable or perceived as normal. A mother-bonded man is seen to give control of his own life to his mother, in exchange for a sense of security. If the mother has more than one son, then she will have, at the most, one mother's boy, usually the eldest son. The relationship between mother and mother's boy is thought to be 'symbiotic': the mother enjoys controlling her mother's boy' - *http://en.wikipedia.org/wiki/Mother's_boy*

Any woman who marries such a 'mama's boy' needs to do some extra work, especially in trying to please the mother-in-law all the time. We shall see how this type of marriage can work.

In the book of Ruth 1, we were told that Naomi's husband died while they were in a sojourner's strange country called Moab, because there was famine in Israel. Her husband's death left her with two sons, Mahlon and Chilion. Both of them took wives from Moab and lived together until these two sons also died and Naomi became a childless widow. From this story we would discover that, as is evident in Ruth 2-4, that Naomi was closer to her sons when she lost her husband, which made him have a closer relationship with their wives.

CHAPTER NINE

In Ruth 1:16-17, Ruth, one of Naomi's daughters-in-law refused to return to her people – she desired to follow Naomi all the days of her life. Now the kind of relationship that existed between them is well explained in Ruth 4:15. The neighbours could testify of Ruth in their own words:

14 Then the women said to Naomi, 'Blessed be the LORD, who has not left you this day without a close relative; and may his name be famous in Israel!

15 And may he be to you a restorer of life and a nourisher of your old age; for your daughter-in-law, who loves you, who is better to you than seven sons, has borne him.'

Ruth to them was better than seven sons – This attribute of Ruth being equated to seven sons was not born in her overnight. It took her years of learning and unlearning - understanding Naomi and her predicament, knowing what her two sons meant to her and voluntarily replacing them and superseding them. When you have a mother-in-law who is so attached to her son, you should be prepared to be that son - know your mother-in-law inside-out, her fears and her secrets.

The Bible made it clear that for two people to walk together, they must agree (Amos 3:3). The symbiotic relationship mother and son have together is 'false passion' oriented. They are together in this relationship, securing their future in each other's fears and hopes. This will be better

CHAPTER NINE

understood when I talk about the case for children in subsequent teaching.

As a wife you must try to understand that your husband is so close to his mother because he finds spiritual regeneration, health, safety and the security of his secrets in her. The secret they share is the reason they are alive and they will often do anything to protect that secret. The mother knows the weakness of her son, and her fear is what will become of him when the wife is aware of this weakness. In situations where the son is the breadwinner, you must let her know that you care even more than her son.

This you can achieve by asking after her often. Phone calls can do the job - you can buy her a phone - and make sure she visits and spends some time with you. Ask her often for advice on how to run the home. She also wants to be a teacher, and has a lot of knowledge that she is willing to let out to a willing daughter-in-law. Do consult her sometimes when the son, your husband, is sick - she knew all about her son and his illnesses before you married him.

Do not forget that many mothers are not happy when they see you cooking food they feel is expensive, especially for mothers who raised their children by feeding them hand to mouth, the kind of home many of us grew up in. Tell your mother-in-law to teach you how to cook some type of food - once she is in the house, beg her to teach you the native

CHAPTER NINE

dishes your husband used to like when he was her young son growing up. Let her tell you stories of how the child went to school - she wants you to see her feelings and what she endured in her marriage while raising your husband.

This is why you need to spend some time with her so that you can have a good understanding of who she is. If your mother-in-law is old, you can talk to your husband and get a home help for her who will assist her in the house. For widows, you must do the extraordinary - she must not be abandoned. If your mother-in-law is ill at the same time as your mother is ill, you had better attend to your mother-in-law first. Your mother will understand, but your mother-in-law will not.

Prove to your mother-in-law that you are ready to join forces with her to ensure her son succeeds. She will come looking for you always. She will live to bless you and your children. Your mother-in-law can do a lot to put a smile on your face as you journey through this unending training of life. She has gone through it and knows better where the shoe pinches - She understands her son much better than you. The story of Rebecca in Genesis 27 is enough to tell us that a mother can go to any extent to ensure that she secures the future of the son she cherishes and loves.

This is why it is not Christianly right for any lady to jump into marriage on the face value of the man alone. You are

CHAPTER NINE

from different worlds. While you are courting, let him tell you much about himself - visit his home, get to know his mother and his family. If his mother is aggressive to you, be careful, and if you must stick to the man, prayerfully seek God's consent. Let God know what you desire and he will surely tell you if the man meets those desires - when I mean desires, I don't mean material satisfaction, I mean a peaceful marriage.

Do not be in a hurry – more haste less speed, they say. Many ladies say 'I loved him when I first saw him', but there is no such thing as love at first sight. You were carried away by the way the man speaks, his dress, his posture etc. So take your time. God is not in a hurry, so don't hurry him either. It took God many thousands of years before he sent his son as a testimony of the love He had for the world. Love comes through development - forget that love you saw at first sight, your mother-in-law is better placed to tell her son 'I love you' because they have known each other for years.

For the men, you can help reduce this mother-in-law/wife friction by the way you intervene. You cannot separate them and they cannot exist independently, because if you try to do so, you will be the one who will suffer most as they continuously contend for your attention, and I assure you it may take your life.

A successful man is a man who creates the environment for his mother and his wife to live like daughter and mother.

CHAPTER NINE

This is about your life - you must find a way. And the best way is to allow your wife more information about you than your mother - open up. Do not gossip about your wife to your mother and vice versa. They both need you.

Men should ensure that their mother is in good tune with their father, if he is alive. No man should support his mother and make her believe you have come to replace his father, her husband. If the mother loves her husband, and if a widow loves her husband, she will not interfere in the marriage affairs of their sons. They will love their daughters-in-law even more.

A man can also settle this matter before his marriage by letting God in from his young years. I was so attached to my mother that my father would tell her not to tell me when they quarrelled. I supported her in all she did and reported my father to her always. While I was not yet born again, I relied on my mother to stop any relationship I wanted stopped, and it worked for me. Then when I became born again, I needed a woman who could replace my mother. As far as I was concerned, that was my problem - I solved it by praying to God for a woman who had a similar character as my mother. My wife is a replica of my mother.

Coping with sisters-in-law
Sisters-in-law often rely on the relationship that existed between them and their brothers while they were growing, as

CHAPTER NINE

a yardstick to attract their brothers' attention. The story of Miriam's hatred for Moses, her brother, in the Bible started when Miriam started having a problem with Moses' wife. She was not happy that Moses was married to a woman who was not a Jew: *'And Miriam and Aaron spake against Moses because of the Ethiopian woman whom he had married: for he had married an Ethiopian woman'* (Numbers 12:1). She began to rebel against Moses inwardly, as well as his wife, and became very sarcastic and ill-natured. Out of jealousy, Miriam joined Aaron and they began to gossip about Moses' marriage to an Ethiopian women: *'Has the Lord spoken only through Moses? Hasn't he also spoken through us?'* - Numbers 12:2.

Sisters-in-law have the capacity to cause havoc in marriages. From the Miriam story, it becomes necessary to look at the early relationship that existed between her and her brother Moses. In the book of Exodus 2:4-8 we are told that Miriam was appointed as chief security officer to Moses, a would-be leader. It was Miriam who gave her mother the employment of bringing Moses up, making her a breadwinner. Her leadership role, in Exodus 15 - leading the women in singing, cannot be under estimated. In Micah 6:4 God recognised her leadership role in the emancipation of the Israelites from the land of Egypt.

Miriam's hatred for Moses grew out of the feeling within her that she was losing him to his wife, Zipporah. Remember that Zipporah never left Egypt with them because Moses had sent her and their two sons back to Midian, to stay with his father in-law, so as to answer God's call - to deliver the Israelites (Exodus 18). The sudden appearance of Zipporah and her two sons as recorded in Exodus 18 was the bone of contention - it is natural that Moses became closer to his wife and children after a 'long time no see' period - this was the trouble in her heart.

This story tells us that Zipporah was never loved by Miriam, which must have caused a lot of trouble in her marriage. A good sister-in-law should encourage her brother's wife. A man should be happy and grateful to God for finding a woman who said yes to his marriage proposal, and sisters-in-law must recognise this fact. Men who have a poor home upbringing often bring shame to the family. Many women sacrifices their goals and ambitions to ensure their husbands' success, so any sister-in-law who is attacking her brother's wife is evil and from the pit of hell - her aim is to destroy God's anointed institution, and she will surely receive her reward. Did Zipporah answer Miriam? No! She never did else the Bible would have also captured that, but God dealt with Miriam His own way.

A woman can sustain her marriage by loving her sisters-in-law. In most cases, men do warn their wives not to be too close to their sisters. This is a lie, they will gang up against

CHAPTER NINE

you, but if you show in-laws love, they will stand to defend you anywhere, any time, except in cases when these in-laws are out to drain the pocket of your husband. The love they seem to have for their brother in most cases is targeted at the man's finance which they feel you are not letting him spend on them. Don't forget your sisters-in-law share a blood feeling with your husband - they are from the same womb and they love each other - forget the game of hatred they display in public sometimes. When the chips are down, you will see them re-grouping as brothers and sisters. The game here is - love her and let her know you care. Call her on the phone and talk to her, pray with her and encourage her.

In many cases, because of fear of losing their brothers, they try to ensure that their brother gets married to a friend, so they can have access to him at any time - so when you show up out of the blue all in the name of their brother's proposal to you they will want to join forces with their mothers to ensure the marriage never works. Use your common sense. Don't fight her or hate her - no matter what happens, try to win them over if you can. Let them know that they have free access to their brother, your would-be husband, during courtship, and after the marriage do not lock your door to them. If they know you are the bridge linking them to their brother they will love you and pave the way for you to enter more into your husband's heart. They will tell you many secrets you don't know - I bet you they will be good at that.

CHAPTER NINE

Many men create an unhealthy environment so that they can misbehave and have nobody to blame them. A man may paint his wife bad before his family and when he discovers that they do not like her any more, he goes out womanizing. If you have been good to your in-laws, they will fight your husband and make life unbearable for him until he returns home and takes care of his responsibilities. The key here is - never hate your sisters-in-law, because they can give you the key to your husband's heart.

Every man who loves his family will ensure there is no rancour between his wife and his family. The leprosy affliction on Miriam was as a result of her hatred for her brother's wife, which led to her addressing Moses with disrespect. When a sister-in-law hates her brother's wife, she talks to her brother with disrespect. As a man you must not allow this to happen - you are the man in the house and must take hold of your family and must speak the language that all parties understand (Esther 1:22). Don't take sides - don't make life unbearable for your wife. She never committed any crime accepting you as a husband. Remember your relations - don't forget them now that you are married if you have been close to them. You need to be closer to them now that you are married. A phone call can allay their fears so that they do not see the coming of your wife as the reason for your distance from them and at the same time do not forget how you begged your wife before she said 'YES'. You need to be a man - a real man.

CHAPTER NINE

Many sisters-in-law like to turn their mother's heart against her daughter in-law. Every wife should sincerely submit to her husband and treat her mother-in-law nicely and she will discover that her sisters-in-law have no basis to attack you any more, rather they will come relying on you to bring them closer to their brother, your husband. And sisters-in-law should stop thinking that their brother's wife is responsible any time they make demands that their brother refuses to honour.

The only advice I want to give to every wife here is that no matter the challenges you are facing from your in-laws or your husband as a result of their evil manipulation against you, the Lord of Hosts who instituted marriage will surely defend you. He defended Sarah twice even when her husband, Abraham, rejected her when he should have been there for her, on the flimsy excuse that they would kill him, but he staked his neck for his nephew Lot when they held him in captivity (Genesis 12:13-18, 20:2-4, 14:14-16). He defended Rebecca by making Abimelech see them when they were playing with each other, after her husband, Isaac, had denied her, so that Abimelech or any other would have molested her sexually (Genesis 26:7-11). He defended Zipporah when Miriam attacked Moses because of her (Numbers 12). And don't forget how He defended Mary, the mother of Jesus when her betrothal husband, Joseph, wanted to secretly put her away (Matthew 1:18-20). Marriage is of

God. Hand over your marriage to Him and any in-law who torments his/her brother's wife will certainly see the wrath of God. 'Let no man put asunder' is God's command. Your reply to they who hunt you is simply: 'The Lord judge between you and me.' - Genesis 16:5.

In all, do not despise your husband. St Peter admired Sarah's submission to Abraham, her husband, which may have fortified and consolidated their marriage from enemy attack: 'Sarah obeyed Abraham, calling him lord, whose daughters you are if you do good and are not afraid with any terror' (I Peter 3:6). As a wife, all you need is not to be afraid of them. Build your home and stay in your home. Call the Lord of Host to duty when you are tormented.

Understand your husband
To understand every man, I want us to go back to the beginning of his existence so that we can derive the characteristics of the being called man from first principles. This information is contained in Genesis chapter 2:8-12:

8 And the LORD God planted a garden eastward in Eden; and there he put the man whom he had formed.

9 And out of the ground made the LORD God to grow every tree that is pleasant to the sight, and good for food; the tree of life also in the midst of the garden, and the tree of knowledge of good and evil.

CHAPTER NINE

10 And a river went out of Eden to water the garden; and from thence it was parted, and became into four heads.

11 The name of the first is Pison: that is it which compasseth the whole land of Havilah, where there is gold;

12 And the gold of that land is good: there is bdellium and the onyx stone.

From the verses we just read, we can see that Adam had a home and his first environment was a beautiful garden called Eden and in this garden were wonderful trees, which were not only beautiful but good for food. There was also the tree of life and the tree of the knowledge of good and evil. To crown it, there were rivers, and one of them flowed through a land full of gold. Eden presented man with ample opportunities to live a life of discovery.

During courtship men often present the following gifts to the woman they love:

1. Beautiful flowers.
2. Perfume, deodorants, sweet aroma body cream.
3. Jewelleries, gold wristwatches.
4. Colourful and vibrant clothes.
5. Good shoes and handbags, etc.

They also appreciate good hairstyles and vibrant dressings - you will notice remarks like 'I love this hairstyle' or 'I love

CHAPTER NINE

your clothes', etc. Occasionally they may dictate the type of hairstyle and the type of clothes they want their lady to wear to certain occasion. This is his standard - he is gradually telling you what he likes; a beautiful good-looking woman, the desire of every man.

In African traditional marriage, and I guess in many parts of the world where traditional marriage is still practised, on the day of the marriage the bride is presented to the groom and the public as a beautiful queen - well dressed in the most expensive traditional costume. Even in a white wedding, the bride's appearance is not compromised. This is the standard the man wants to see thereafter - a colourful, elegant and charming queen.

In the book of Esther 1:11-12, Queen Vashti's refusal to display her beauty as a mark of honour to her husband led to the end of her marriage. Men value honour, and their pride is their wife. They want to see her as a beautiful wife, but not a shameless harlot. Many married women today dress like harlots, exposing their nakedness in public - these women should desist from whore-like clothing, as they cause their husband even more pain, though they may allow the sleeping dogs to lie for a while.

No wife should think that her husband will accept anything less from what he saw in her that attracted him to her. Those flowers, perfumes, creams and other gifts he bought while you were courting were his specifications and you must know this.

Adam saw in Eve a being different from him and another opportunity to discover, this time, the being he gladly called 'woman.' In effect, we were made to understand in Genesis 3:6 that Adam was right there when Eve was being tempted by Satan - Adam was not foolish, he wanted to understand his woman's feelings and was ready to sacrifice eternity for her. This is man for you. For Adam to be right there with his wife means he was proud of his wife. Your husband wants to be proud of you - make him proud, look beautiful. Be sweet smelling and charming.

The following will guide you on how to treat your husband now that you understand his taste:

1. Encourage him to have a good home

The Garden of Eden is Man's original standard of a good home. Many men prefer sleeping in beautiful hotels and feel more comfortable there than in their homes. The reason is because the hotel room and environment is beautiful and neat. Having a good home starts with encouraging him to have his own home - a place he can retire to spend the night and yet be comfortable - not a home in his parents' house, unless the parents are dead and he inherits the house. Living with a man in his parents' home should be discouraged, because there is going to be both cold and hot war all the time.

CHAPTER NINE

2. Keep the home neat and inviting

Some men are carried away when they step into hotels because of the neatness and beauty of the hotel. A neat home always encourages a man to return home. Adam's home was a land filled with gold and precious stones for his use. There were rivers that encompassed the land for him to give enjoyment and freshness. For beauty in the home, select colourful curtains, put out some flowers and keep them neat. Have a good sense of positioning, be creative, add spice to your home by changing your photograph in the sitting room and the bedroom – Don't allow one photograph to stay for months. Also get new photographs of both of you and keep displaying them in strategic positions in the house, where they will easily catch his eye. Do this for your kids also. The bed in the bedroom should be neatly and colourfully dressed. Change the bedspreads and pillow cases often. Your kitchen should be neat and the bathroom and all surroundings should be colourful.

Enticing him

Everything that surrounds a man is his environment, including his home. An environment can be beautiful, pleasant, comfortable or horrible, uncomfortable etc. The following are ways to entice him:

1. Sweet aromas: Resist anything that will bring distance

CHAPTER NINE

between you both. When you are bound close, you don't quarrel. Bad odour kills love. Wear good feminine perfume such as the ones containing pheromones. It has being scientifically proven that pheromones, which are naturally occurring chemicals that send out subconscious scent signals to the opposite sex, cause very powerful sexual arousal and attraction in your husband. There are many of them in the stores, so do a review on the internet before you buy. Use good air fresheners to keep the home inviting all the time.

2. Be very neat: Always remember his original garden in Eden, where we all started from: He likes sweet smells. Some men who have had more than one wife may go after the younger wife because she is neat. Be very neat, shaving the hairs in your armpits. Many a man would want their wife to shave her genitals – you know what I mean. Let your underwear be neat and enticing too.

3. Also help your husband to look neat and sharp – the children too. Help him to be neat, and advise him to shave his beard. You can invite the barber to come home, or follow him to the barber's shop. The children's clothes should be neat and clean too. They must have baths often so that they don't look dirty. Dress them in clothes with attractive colours, so that your husband will always want them around him. Always let the man know when he needs new clothes – A

CHAPTER NINE

man can be wearing the same clothes without complaining until somebody tells him to change them – and when this happens, he will rely on the same person to acknowledge him any time he puts on a new set of clothing. And if the one who told him is a woman, you are losing him already. Again tell him to shave his beard, and be cute looking. Let him wear sharp T-shirts sometimes.

4. Be relevant in your dressing: There are clothes for different occasions, at home, going out etc. When at home, do not appear in rags and say 'who's going to look at me', because you feel you are now married, you are no longer enticing and do not need to keep yourself as young as possible. Sarah was still looking beautiful and striking even at 90 years of age.

5. Don't always take your bath with him – even if you must bath together, let it not be often in order to create a sense of discovery in him. If you always take your bath with him, with time you will discover that he does not touch you or find your body enticing any more, because there is nothing for him to discover - he is too used to you.

No man takes an interest in things he is used to. One example is an old set of electronics. The first time he brings them to the house, you will find him trying out all the buttons, but with time he does not even remember the set exists.

6. Don't always appear nude before him. Many women feel

CHAPTER NINE

that appearing nude before their husband all the time will pull him closer. This is not 100% true. Nudity is not what actually attracts a man. It may do in at first, but after that you may discover he is no longer finding pleasure in your nudity. If you must put on your clothes in his presence do it with style, let him not see your nakedness. This act will spark off his curiosity. Let him discover your nudity for himself – don't push it in his face.

7. When he comes close, fall into his arms, and if he fondles your body, don't stop him – be careful not to raise the adrenaline hormone level in him - talk to him softly, allowing his sexual desire to build up. Hold him close and ensure you smell really good. Look into his eyes when he is talking. Limit talking with him from a distance when together – talk to him close up, nose to nose, eyes to eyes, forehead to forehead, mouth to mouth. Hug him almost every moment of the day – your head on his chest - head between the breast for close talking. Your breath, odour, mouth smell, could be a repellent, which you must work on.

8. Make it a duty to spend time together alone on the balcony with him in the day or night. In Genesis 26:8, Abimelech saw Isaac and Rebecca having a good time together, meaning that they were playing as lovers. As always, ensure your hair does not smell, wear nice perfumes, take your bath, wear a good

CHAPTER NINE

dress and stay with him. Encourage family time out with the children and while they are playing. Sometimes both of you should sit the children down and teach them – do not do it alone. Don't make him feel you can exist without him, ever.

9. Speak softly: Don't appear to nag. A soft voice turns away anger. Do not talk like a man. Talking like a man is seen as challenge and he will resist it with his blood. Even when he keeps quiet, he will sometimes pay you back – you attend to a child who speaks helplessly – don't give him the impression that you think you are the man in the house.

10. Use the magic of your eyes. The eyes of a woman are different from those of a man. The Bible says of Rachael in Genesis 29:17 that she has beautiful tender eyes. Know how to caress him with your eyes. Let him become helpless under the power of your seductive eyes. With dull, loving eyes, seemingly looking helpless, take him to your dreamland of love.

11. The place of your underwear: Men sometimes pretend not to bother, especially for those of us who are pastors. Sisters, who often entice pastor into sexual relationships, wear revealing underwear for instance. If you know how to use the power of your underwear, you will see his eyes going towards your brassiere, which holds your breasts, similar to his mother's, which fed him as a toddler. Men love breasts I can tell you this – milk in it or not, they like sucking them. Make your breasts neat and have him suck them in turn.

CHAPTER NINE

To be a decent and disciplined wife, when you are alone with your husband, don't let him see the same old undies you have been wearing for months. Change them often and always put on your underwear to let him be the only one to discover your nudity. As I said before, he is a discoverer, even if he is a pastor, a man is a man. Let your underwear be neat and new looking. New undies spark his erotic sense and you will see him thinking like a man. I shall throw more light on this when I talk about how to create the passion display environment.

12. Avoid smelling of milk when you are breast feeding: Many men have been complaining of their wives smelling of milk when they are breastfeeding a new baby. In this case, you should get closer to your husband immediately after your bath. In the Bible, when a woman delivers she is allowed to stay in her tent until her period of purification is over. In our modern society this is no longer practised, but you can limit the breastfeeding period by using a breast pump so that you can spend some time with your husband.

13. Limit the habit of riding in separate cars: driving takes more of your thinking because you are always on alert, and when the car breaks down you are going to have a bad day. You should always be together. If this is not going to be possible, then at least once or twice a week, ride together, and when you are together don't fail to look your best – He wants

to be proud of you. If he does not want you to visit friends or relatives together, and this is common, then he is ashamed of you. Change your looks, let him see you as a brand new fire shining like the morning sun, and you will see him coming to get warmed up in your arms.

14. Understand his spiritual inclinations – encourage him to pick up a role in the church and start a ministry, after prayerfully waiting on God. At weekends you can decide to visit orphanages. If you are blessed financially, encourage him to start a foundation to help people with needs. Man was kept in the garden to care for it. Every man has a job to do for God – every man has a ministry. The more you work together in God's vineyard, the more you will be able to keep on enticing him, because he will become all yours.

Creating the passion display environment

To conclude this chapter we will get some basic facts from Proverbs 7:13-22, which is a warning against the adulteress. For the married woman who is enticing her husband, this is no sin. The offensive elements in these verses will be removed, to help us drive home our point vividly on how you could create the passion display environment:

13 So she caught him, and kissed him, and with an impudent face said unto him,

CHAPTER NINE

14 I have peace offerings with me; this day have I paid my vows.

15 Therefore came I forth to meet thee, diligently to seek thy face, and I have found thee.

16 I have decked my bed with coverings of tapestry, with carved works, with fine linen of Egypt.

17 I have perfumed my bed with myrrh, aloes, and cinnamon.

18 Come, let us take our fill of love until the morning: let us solace ourselves with loves.

19 For the goodman is not at home, he is gone a long journey:

20 He hath taken a bag of money with him, and will come home at the day appointed.

21 With her much fair speech she caused him to yield, with the flattering of her lips she forced him.

22 He goeth after her straightway, as an ox goeth to the slaughter.

From this passage, we learn the following:

Verse 13: Every woman should know how to meet her husband, kiss him and talk to him. However, since she is not an adulterous woman, she should use a soft tone, and with a smile on her face persuade her husband to listen to her.

Verse 14: We can liken the peace offering and the vow she paid to the wife's relationship with God. The context

CHAPTER NINE

would read, 'I am born again, and I am in good standing with God, and it gladdens my heart to tell you that I will make heaven if the trumpet sounds now.' Every woman should desire to be in Christ, because He is our peace. Her vows should be her ability to stand firm in her faith.

Verse 15: The word there is how she desired the man – diligently. This should show in the action and not in the saying. Every husband wants to be assured that the woman has no life elsewhere. Even I as a pastor have found husbands ask me what relationship I have with their wives, and why they keep on calling me.

Verse 16: The bed must be well made with quality linen. Get a blanket rolled at the foot. You can actually visit a five star hotel to see how the beds are done. Remember that man was created and kept in a wonderful environment. As someone who is fearfully and wonderfully made, he wants to sleep in a lovely bed. Don't forget that your husband wants to discover something new always. Keep him in suspense and you will discover that his appetite for food and sexual intimacy will improve.

Verse 17: This is self explanatory. Perfume the bed.

Verse 18: Invite him to bed. Don't be totally naked. You should have applied a moisturising cream. Let the light in the room be a little dim, as men are often shy. Be careful not to arouse his adrenalin, but keep his serotonin and melatonin working. Don't demand money. Look into his eyes and let him know that he is safe. Every man wants this assurance of safety. They are often afraid of death, thinking that they might lose their wife to someone else when they die. Men are possessive. Know this!

Verse 19-20: No one is allowed to disturb you. Make sure both of you are alone in your paradise. The environment should be calm. Birds may sing if you like. There should be no sweat on you. Your armpits should be well taken care of. Allow a little finger-nail growth on the fingers you will use to tickle him - you know what I mean!

The last two verses say that the man responded, so your husband should respond also, if you know where to touch. You don't need fasting and prayers to do all these.

CHAPTER TEN

THE CASE FOR SEX

Sex is simply the joining of the male and female sex organs, the penis into the vagina. There is evidence that humans learned sex from animals. When God created Adam, before he lost the rib which later became his wife, he never had sex. The animals too were not in the garden but in the field. The garden was like a courtroom, or would also be seen as an administrative unit for the world. So God had to bring the animals to him to name them, then they would go back into the field, where they grazed and reproduced.

Even when the woman came into being, they still never had sex until God said that the woman would bring forth in pain. There and then it dawned on Adam that his wife was the avenue through which procreation was possible, and he changed her name to Eve. That happened to be their last moment in that garden, and they left to go into an unknown environment, the field which was the habitat of the beasts. While there men started living in fear, and had to learn how to survive in that wild forest. Man started eating all manner

CHAPTER TEN

of fruits, leaves and animals, making him an omnivore. This wasn't so in the garden. Man learned all manner of survival tricks from the animals. There also they saw the animals having sexual intercourse, and man tried out what they saw, and the Bible said: 'and Adam knew his wife.'

We see that Adam never asked God how they should procreate. Today we are not surprised that sexual sin is predominant in our lives until one has Christ. Sexual urge decays as one becomes close to God and grows with Him. Adultery and multiple sex partners are all the practices of animals. Cohabitation is also the practice of animals –animals don't marry. We should not be surprised that today we have so many sex styles which resemble what animals do: the doggy position, the monkey position, the dragon position etc. An unbeliever practises all manner of sex moves, including body licking, just as dogs do, which many believers have now got used to because of their previous experience in the world.

Now that we understand the origin of most of our sexual practices, I think the wise person would want to discipline him/herself to please God even as we engage in sex in our marriages. As we go on into this discussion, the following will become clear.

- What is sex? – The act of copulation.
- Purpose of sex – God designed it mainly for reproduction.
- Who should have sex? – Only the married.

CHAPTER TEN

- How best to enjoy sex – As pleasing to both, but acceptable unto God.
- What are evil sex practices? – Sexual acts that are dehumanizing.

Before we go further into other areas of sex, let us take the following Bible verses from Leviticus to heart:

10 If a man commits adultery with another man's wife— with the wife of his neighbour— both the adulterer and the adulteress must be put to death.

11 If a man sleeps with his father's wife, he has dishonoured his father. Both the man and the woman must be put to death; their blood will be on their own heads.

12 If a man sleeps with his daughter-in-law, both of them must be put to death. What they have done is a perversion; their blood will be on their own heads.

13 If a man lies with a man as one lies with a woman, both of them have done what is detestable. They must be put to death; their blood will be on their own heads.

14 If a man marries both a woman and her mother, it is wicked. Both he and they must be burned in the fire, so that no wickedness will be among you.

15 If a man has sexual relations with an animal, he must be put to death, and you must kill the animal.

CHAPTER TEN

16 If a woman approaches an animal to have sexual relations with it, kill both the woman and the animal. They must be put to death; their blood will be on their own heads.

17 If a man marries his sister, the daughter of either his father or his mother, and they have sexual relations, it is a disgrace. They must be cut off before the eyes of their people. He has dishonoured his sister and will be held responsible.

18 If a man lies with a woman during her monthly period and has sexual relations with her, he has exposed the source of her flow, and she has also uncovered it. Both of them must be cut off from their people.

19 Do not have sexual relations with the sister of either your mother or your father, for that would dishonour a close relative; both of you would be held responsible.

20 If a man sleeps with his aunt, he has dishonoured his uncle. They will be held responsible; they will die childless.

21 If a man marries his brother's wife, it is an act of impurity; he has dishonoured his brother. They will be childless.

22 Keep all my decrees and laws and follow them, so that the land where I am bringing you to live may not vomit you out.

23 You must not live according to the customs of the nations I am going to drive out before you. Because they did all these things, I abhorred them. Leviticus 20:10-23

CHAPTER TEN

Thus saith the LORD, Learn not the way of the heathen - Jeremiah 10:2

Even as Sodom and Gomorrah, and the cities about them in like manner, giving themselves over to fornication, and going after strange flesh, are set forth for an example, suffering the vengeance of eternal fire. - Jude 1:7

If the servants of God would consecrate themselves and avoid strange sex, and those they are sent to are yet to be consecrated, then we would keep on living as though we are orphans. All evil sexual acts are carried out by wild people – and that tells us something. No one who engages in these forms of sex can truly claim to be an image and likeness of God. The world needs healing and deliverance from the claws of the devil. I can't imagine telling my aged parents that I have oral sex with my wife, for instance, not to mention letting God know, which He already does while I am in the act. If we believe that our marriage is consecrated and dedicated to God, we should also carry out the sexual act in the way it ought to be. We must have a change of heart. If any part of your body makes you sin, then it is better to get that part subdued through the word of God. Speak to that part of your body and it would respond to your decree.

How will you look upon your pastor, ministering early in the morning on the pulpit after sucking a vulva, or sipping the vaginal fluid with his tongue? Or how can you look at a female music director singing in a service after she has swallowed sperm? We may argue that, healthwise, we have washed ourselves clean, but God sees us. Our body is His temple. I don't expect anyone to argue this. I know in my spirit that something is wrong with oral sex. The God I serve cannot be mocked. Even now, many ministers are saying that fasting cannot stop sex. We can go on and on praying, but God will not be mocked, we must change our hearts. David said, create in me a clean heart – a heart that will not think of lesbianism, gay sex, oral sex, gang sex, phone sex, etc but a heart that fears God – Psalms 51:10. Seek salvation with trembling and fear.

Immoral sexual acts

Immoral sexual acts include fornication, adultery, gay sex, lesbianism, oral sex etc. Any sexual act in marriage or out of marriage that God will frown at is immoral. Many would still argue that oral sex itself is not wrong because the Bible didn't specifically say so, but anything that goes against God's divine purpose is indeed wrong. Sex is between the sexual organs. Inasmuch as we do not put food into our genitals, there should be no reason to use the mouth for what is made for the genitals. If we examine God's ordained laws and principles, commonplace in the Bible, we see that sexual immorality is not overlooked by God.

CHAPTER TEN

Thou hast also committed fornication with the Egyptians thy neighbours, great of flesh; and hast increased thy whoredoms, to provoke me to anger - Ezekiel 16:26

Mortify therefore your members which are upon the earth; fornication, uncleanness, inordinate affection, evil concupiscence, and covetousness, which is idolatry - Colossians 3:5

Many people are living in sin, all in the name of being justified by faith. How can we have faith when we are not in good standing with God? We cannot create our own laws but to understand the laws of God and uphold them. The Bible says: *For ye know what commandments we gave you by the Lord Jesus. For this is the will of God, even your sanctification, that ye should abstain from fornication: That every one of you should know how to possess his vessel in sanctification and honour; Not in the lust of concupiscence, even as the Gentiles which know not God* - 1 Thessalonians 4:2-5

Immoral sexual acts include immoderate affection, evil concupiscence and covetousness or lust of concupiscence. Enjoying sexual pleasures that will provoke the Lord to anger is sin. Many married couples say that oral sex is helping them to fulfil their marital obligations to the fullest in that they are now able to satisfy each other's libido. Can anyone really think that oral sex can help married couples to have peace in their homes? I don't think so!

When we indulge in any form of sexual immorality,

CHAPTER TEN

whether or not wife and husband, we invite the spirit of devil into our relationship, and then we are tempted again and again until we become drained, in and out, by sexual dissatisfaction.

The term 'oral sex' involves using the tongue on the sexual organs. This sexual act is an activity that involves the stimulation of the genitalia of a sex partner by the use of the mouth, tongue, teeth or throat. Cunnilingus refers to oral sex performed on females, while fellatio refers to oral sex performed on males. Anilingus refers to oral stimulation of a person's anus. Oral stimulation of other parts of the body (as in kissing and licking) is usually not considered oral sex.

This act of oral sex was never found in the Bible, because it was not thought of. Some heathen cultures frown against it, especially in the tribe I hail from, Isoko, in the Niger Delta area of Nigeria. Man was led astray in the beginning by the singular act of not obeying God, but obeying the woman. We need to be closer to God. This is finding more acceptance in the church. This shows that something is definitely wrong somewhere. What are we leaving for God if we are comfortable doing what we used to do outside, before we repented, inside the church? Can we easily tell people that we had oral sex? If we feel so ashamed about it, what do we think God is doing? God said there is a forbidden fruit. Oral sex is a forbidden fruit in sexual relations. Let us obey God for once. Marriage is not an excuse to practise pornography in the house.

Oral sex defeats God's purpose; 'be fruitful and multiply' is

CHAPTER TEN

God's first instruction to man, and there is no way we can multiply through oral sex. One would argue that oral sex does not take the place of sexual intercourse but merely should be part of foreplay. How true is that assumption? It is time we challenged ourselves to show that oral sex was first reported among the children of God or among the early church. Many Christians and non-Christians would love the kind of satisfaction they get from these sensations, especially the women climaxing into orgasm.

Lesbians have refused to repent because they enjoy the sensation they get from oral sex. We must be conscious of the fact that not everything that feels good and looks good to us is right. The Bible warns in Proverbs 14:12: *There is a way which seemeth right unto a man, but the end thereof are the ways of death.* And in Proverbs 16:2, the Bible also says: *All the ways of a man are clean in his own eyes; but the LORD weigheth the spirits.*

If we want to be victorious Christians we have to go after Biblical principles. Let's take a look at the following verses:

Love not the world, neither the things that are in the world. If any man love the world, the love of the Father is not in him. The world today is going after this kind of life. Ask yourself why the doubt in Christians heart about oral sex, where is it commonly found? - 1John 2:15

Because straight is the gate, and narrow is the way, which leadeth unto life, and few there be that find it. - Matthew 7:14

So the last shall be first, and the first last: for many be called, but few chosen. - Matthew 20:16

CHAPTER TEN

And it came to pass, when God destroyed the cities of the plain, that God remembered Abraham, and sent Lot out of the midst of the overthrow, when he overthrew the cities in the which Lot dwelt. - Genesis 19:29

And spared not the old world, but saved Noah the eighth person, a preacher of righteousness, bringing in the flood upon the world of the ungodly -2 Peter 2:5

These verses of the Bible paint a picture of what God is interested in – not what pleases everybody, but what pleases Him. The mere fact that other believers see an act as good does not make it good in the sight of God. Let us be guided.

Oral sex, anal sex, lesbianism, etc are the fulfilment of the desires of the flesh. Revelations 12 told us that this world is under the government of the devil. The book of 2 Corinthians 4:4 says: *In whom the god of this world hath blinded the minds of them which believe not...* Also, John 14:30 Jesus has this to say: *Hereafter I will not talk much with you: for the prince of this world cometh...*

What these imply is that the evil sexual practices that we indulge ourselves in are the manipulation of the devil, and especially through the influence of the mermaid spirit.

And be not conformed to this world: but be ye transformed by the renewing of your mind, that ye may prove what is that good, and acceptable, and perfect, will of God. - Romans 12:2

Biblically, moral justification that approves an act to be carried out and acceptable to our faith is seen below:

CHAPTER TEN

- If it is forbidden, it is a no go.
- If it is not mentioned, be careful, but use discretion.
- If it is approved, do it, yet with caution.

In interpersonal sexual conduct, natural copulation is specified. Kissing mouth-to-mouth is specified - Song of Solomon 1:2: *Let him kiss me with the kisses of his mouth: for thy love is better than wine.* Fondling and sucking of the wife's breasts is specified- Proverbs 5:18-19: *Let thy fountain be blessed: and rejoice with the wife of thy youth. [Let her be as] the loving hind and pleasant roe; let her breasts satisfy thee at all times; and be thou ravished always with her love.*

Other sexually-stimulating conduct is either forbidden or not mentioned. Therefore, other means of sexual stimulation by one person to another is not approved.

As for anal sex, the anus is for faeces. So no one would argue that. It is only in birds that we see that the anus and the vagina are connected. But humans are not birds. This is what the homosexuals do, why do we have to imitate them? God frowned at anal sex in Sodom and Gomorrah, and He destroyed the city.

Sex was mainly made for reproduction, though the pleasure we usually attain from sexual intercourse is an enticement that would make us go into it often, even when the woman is pregnant already. The purpose of sexual intercourse is not to provide pleasure but to enable us bring forth offspring. There

CHAPTER TEN

is more and more evidence of health risks from oral-genital stimulation.

Christians are not to engage in unnecessary activity that harms the body, which is the temple of the Holy Spirit. This is why we also advise Christians not to take alcohol and smoke cigarettes. Many have claimed, as said earlier, that oral-genital stimulation gives them satisfaction, and many doctors have advised thus. This does not necessarily give pleasure, it is the mind set of those involve. And since it doesn't lead to reproduction, which is what God intended sex for, it should be detested.

In everything we do, we need to look at the consequences. Many of us cry in our prayers, believing that God has not forgiven us because of the flashback memory of the acts we commit in private. We should not be seen as sowing seeds of action that will grow into trees of shame in our lives. It is time to call a spade a spade. Sex is between the genital organs – Keep it so. Nothing more, nothing less. I pray that God in His mercy, which abounds forever, would reveal to you the secret in these words of sanctification which you have just read. Jesus says in John 17:17 – *Sanctify them with your truth, your word is truth.*

CHAPTER ELEVEN

THE CASE FOR CHILDREN

The purpose of sex is for child bearing. The Bible tells us that what brings a child to life is the process of the husband knowing the wife. Biology has analyzed the process as involving the release of cells from each of them to form a cell that would become the child. This child then carries traits of the father and mother, spiritually and physically. This implies that the warmth the family experiences as a result of the coming into the family of the child is more to do with watching themselves grow up again, with the characters and habits they had heard stories about, when their mum and dad told them what they used to do when they were growing up.

My mother came into the maternity ward where my wife lay after given birth to my son, and when she took the baby up, she exclaimed: 'This is my son, I could remember when I gave birth to his father – he was just like this.' One could see the joy in her heart as she thought back 37 years. This is the kind of joy that a child brings into the home.

CHAPTER ELEVEN

When no child is on the way
Many marriages have shattered because of the absence of children. In most, the trouble has been directed towards the woman. This has also given the attackers of marriages – mothers-in-law, sisters-in-law and their like - to subject the woman to untold agony.

The importance of children cannot be overlooked. Even at that, we shouldn't forget that Abraham and Sarah had to believe God for years before they had the promised heir. Many marriages today are breaking up because of lack of children. In some homes, the lack of one sex has also rendered many marriages broken. My mother married my father in 1964, and they had me in 1972. During these years of childlessness, my mother recounted how my father's sister would throw my mother's bags and baggage out of his house. She recounted also the humiliation she went through at the hands of traditional medical practitioners and spiritualists, who had to tell her lots of fables as a means of sustaining her patronage.

Through these years, she learned that the only support a woman needs is the love of her husband. Maybe, borrowing from Sarah's action in the Bible, she had to get my father another wife who bore him my elder sister. She also recounted how she almost became a slave to my father's relatives, all to ensure she kept her marriage.

As she recounted her stories, the occasional tremble she

CHAPTER ELEVEN

gave made me imagine the height of pain she must have gone through. Any time I see a full moon hanging in the sky, I always remember how she had sat me down at the age of ten to tell me the ordeal she went through as a barren woman. This has also prompted me to search the scriptures to find out if having children is a must. And indeed, while God gives children, I have learned in the scriptures that having children is a thing of choice. Jesus made us to know that some would indeed become eunuchs for the sake of the gospel - Matthew 19:12.

Couples should not feel as if the world is going to fall on them if they don't bear children. It is not a must that we must bear children in marriage. I don't really attach so much importance to child bearing. What is of more concern to me is how to bring them up to a standard approved by God, where the children would serve Him all the days of their lives. See this concern as God talked about what He feels in His heart that Abraham will surely do for Him:

17 Then the Lord said, 'Shall I hide from Abraham what I am about to do? 18 Abraham will surely become a great and powerful nation, and all nations on earth will be blessed through him. 19 For I have chosen him, so that he will direct his children and his household after him to keep the way of the Lord by doing what is right and just, so that the Lord will bring about for Abraham what he has promised him. – Genesis 18:17-19

CHAPTER ELEVEN

Significance of a child's birth

The birth of Jesus is our example here. A star appeared in heaven when he was born. The book of Psalms 127:3 says that children are a gift of God and the fruit of the womb is His reward. The male sex is highly valued among Africans and many other nations, while the absence of boys is regarded as the possible extermination of a lineage, especially when the couple have no other hope of another child as in the case of Abraham and Sarah (Genesis 16:2). Biblical events related to the birth of a child shows that as soon as the child was brought to life it was washed in a bath, rubbed with salt and wrapped in swaddling clothes, Ezekiel 16:4; Luke 2:7.

As captured in Luke 2:22, the name is given to the child on the 8th day. The rite of circumcision is performed on the male child on this same day. The child is then nursed by the mother up to about three years or when he/she is older. The father takes more interest in the upbringing of the male, while the woman does same for the female, explaining why the Bible says *Train up a child in the way he should go: and when he is old, he will not depart from it.* – Proverbs 22:6.

Training the child

Training the child starts from conception. Samuel was weaned by the mother before sending him to Eli. Moses was trained up by his mother after he was entrusted under her care by

CHAPTER ELEVEN

Pharaoh's daughter. For Pharaoh's daughter to accept Miriam's proposal for her mother to wean Moses shows that the princess confirmed through the calibre of whom the mother was that she could actually take care of little Moses.

Pregnant women know what joy they feel when the child kicks in their womb. Christian mothers also know that during this period you can actually communicate with the baby. In our own case we knew what our babies would look like before we had it. They appeared to us in dreams, and the names we called them are the names they answered in my dreams. To be able to train up a child, we must know who they would become. This is always the case in the Bible, where the names of children finally link to the lives they will live after birth.

This therefore means that apart from the physical training and instructions we give them as they grow, their names act as a remote control to bring them to an expected end defined identity.

All of us are children of our parents and we know how our presence, characters, behaviour and the associations we kept affected their marriage. For instance because of my attitude when my mother chastised me, my father would start a real quarrel with my mother and hit her hard. I was happy, because I felt my father loved me, but only on the day in 2007 when I told him I used to smoke did he know that his protective nature of me would have ruined my life if God had not intervened. Some of those I used to smoke with are already dead. I wish I had preached to them rather than joined them in smoking.

Children in most cases determine how much the marriage will grow. They have a role in ensuring a blissful marriage in their home. Children dying before their parents is an anomaly. Who knows, it could be because they refused to honour their parents as commanded in Exodus 20:12, except for infant mortality due to illness.

Parents' duties in raising children
Many women have driven their husbands into bankruptcy because they want to belong to a higher social class, not for the benefit of training a child with good morals and academic intelligence, but to see themselves as measuring up to the dictates of the standards set by a higher class. School fees do not have to be exorbitant for a child to get the best training. School fees in most cases are determined by the greed of the owners.

The average cost of raising a child to the age of eighteen is increasing by the day, and many parents do not have the kind of income that can conveniently cater for the needs of the child. Once children are brought up wrongly they grow up doing evil, with no fear of God in their hearts. Their attitude will also have a negative effect in the marriage, because no father will be happy to have a wayward son or daughter as a child. Fathers pounce on the mother, believing she was responsible for the illness in the family. Women should take raising children a call to duty, bringing up in the fear of the lord. A child should be train the way he should grow.

Tools for raising up children
- Don't spare the rod
- Teach them
- Raise them in the fear of the lord
- Take them out to visit good homes
- Don't take alcohol in their present
- Don't fight mummy in their present

Common mistakes parents make
- Junior takes the father's inheritance syndrome
- Mummy/daddy's pet
- The good child takes after daddy while the bad child takes after the mother syndrome
- Neophilic syndrome – loving the younger child more than the older ones, and finding it difficult to correct the child when he/she does wrong.

Duty of children in sustaining the marriage
Children present an opportunity for both mothers and fathers to correct the wrongs they notice among themselves, because the girl-child in most cases may take after the mother, as the

boy-child takes after the father. What an opportunity to watch a 'video' of your wife or husband growing as a child!

We should tell our children the mistakes that made it difficult for us to achieve certain goals in life which would have made us more successful than we are. Once a marriage is broken, the children are often scattered. Some take sides with daddy or mummy. Children have a duty to play in helping their parents to stay together happily.

The Bible told us that children should honour their parents so that their day would be long. Longevity means long life, and the only way a child can honour his/her parents is when he/she has the fear of God by surrendering his or her life to Jesus.

Since children are an inheritance from God and he who has them is blessed, their conduct in life is important. They are blessed after Him, see Proverbs 20.

Tools needed by any child to develop
- Seek wisdom.
- Avoid bad friends.
- Cook in the house, wash your clothes.
- Have a timetable so that they spend less time watching movies or playing computer games.
- Be involved in church activities.
- Fear God and respect elders.
- Love your studies.

CHAPTER ELEVEN

Common mistakes children make
- Reporting daddy to mummy, and vice versa.
- Being jealous when daddy is with mummy (girls).
- Fighting among themselves.
- Stealing out of the house.
- Hating grandmother because mum and grand mother do not agree. Then they are bound to lose their father's love and care.
- Siding with daddy or mummy when they quarrel.
- Hating daddy or mummy.

The other side
Even why many marriages are dying because of the absence of children, some are being killed by societal vices. Infanticide is the intentional killing of infants, while neonaticide, killing infants within 24 hours of a child's birth, is most commonly done by the mother. In many past societies, as seen in the Bible where baal worshippers had to sacrifice their children, certain forms of infanticide were considered permissible. In some countries, female infanticide is more common than the killing of male offspring, due to sex selection. This points to the fact that child-killing in marriage is to do with the absence of God in these homes.

CHAPTER TWELVE

THE CASE FOR IN-LAWS

As I mentioned earlier, my mother's ordeal was not with my father but her sister-in-law. The man in most cases tends to be more submissive to the demands of his relatives than those of his wife and children, though this act in some men has also been dictated by the behaviour of their wives.

In Africa I have yet to see a man who actually obeyed God in leaving his mother and father to cling to his wife. Now we would see that the heart-rending trouble that Abraham went through was caused by his nephew, Lot. First Lot had servants who disagreed with those of Abraham. The disagreement could be seen as a reflection of the kind of relationship he was having with Abraham. If he had shown total respect, his servants would have also shown that in the field.

Another instance would be when Lot had to take the most beautiful and flourishing part of Jordan, leaving Abraham to ponder over how he was going to survive. The intervention of God would show how he was actually feeling. And again, when Lot was taken captive, Abraham left all he had to go and rescue Lot. If he had died in that war, that would have been the end of the promise of God he was bearing. Looking at the story of Abraham, one would also want to see what God told him in Genesis 12. Abraham disobeyed by not leaving by himself alone but going with Lot.

Another side of the story that disheartened me was why Abraham would deny His wife for fear of being killed, and yet go ahead to rescue Lot from death. Why didn't he use the force he had to defend his wife, at least for once, instead of denying her before her face? This was an act I would rather call 'secular divorce,' which is denying your spouse so as to achieve or secure worldly or material gains. Many men, even in our present dispensation, have allowed their wives to have sex with those they want to favour them. While in the university, I actually heard of a story of a student in one of the universities who sent his fiancée to sleep with his lecturer in order to graduate, because the lecturer opted for that option seeing that the girl was beautiful.

Again I have also seen many women whose brothers would disregard their husbands because their sister seems to earn a good salary. Many women have also used their brothers as their next of kin even when they are married, in the fear that if they die, their husbands would spend whatsoever they had laboured for on a new wife. These are not marriages. A man once complained that his wife locked the bathroom

CHAPTER TWELVE

behind her when she was bathing. This had started since she had been earning a bigger salary, and her family had taken over the control of her life.

This story points to the fact that in our marriages, the influences of the in-laws, whether father in-laws, mother in-laws, brother in-laws and sister in-laws from both parties, if not curtailed, would breed pain for the couples. The reason the man's family won't leave the couple to enjoy their marriage is that they often see the man as a means to an end, especially if he is well off. They see the man as a breadwinner whom they must sacrifice, like a soldier dying for his country. This may be confirmed if the man suddenly dies. The tears they shed and the words they speak will tell you that they see their relationship to their brother as parasitic.

I have seen homes where a man's sisters would leave their own marriage to start staying with their brothers. As long as that is condoned, such shameless women will keep on disrespecting their own husbands, without a thought as to how they could build their own homes to please the Lord. These women hate any pastor who would preach: 'let no man put asunder.' Gradually they will lead their brother into hell, as he will soon start neglecting his own family responsibilities. Any woman married to such a man must be ready to be up and doing, because such men don't usually last long, and sooner than later they will go, leaving the woman to cater for

CHAPTER TWELVE

the children. Then these same shylock in-laws will render them homeless. The fear of the Lord in our heart is the only cure to this.

Miriam, in Numbers 12:1, took the lead, with Aaron, in the complaint against Moses for his marriage to an Ethiopian: *And Miriam and Aaron spake against Moses because of the Ethiopian woman whom he had married: for he had married an Ethiopian woman, and for this sinful act she was attacked with leprosy.* This leprous infection and its removal, which took place at Hazeroth, form the last public event and usefulness to God of Miriam's life (Numbers 12:1-15). She died toward the close of the wanderings at Kadesh, and was buried there without any significant mention of the important role she played in the Israelites' rescue mission (Numbers 20:1).

I want also to talk about how Rebecca was sent forth to her husband. Today we have cultures that will send the family of the woman with her to her husband's house, and in most cases, these people end up being gossips who will expose the home to spiritual cobwebs.

While I prepared to end this topic, in the early hours of Monday 11th June 2012, I received two text messages from my wife which had been sent to her by a sister, and I was wondering why, because I know my wife. None of the accusations she laid were facts, because I have my life to live and my wife was not controlling me to visit home as she

CHAPTER TWELVE

claimed. I am called by God to serve, and if God says I should be going to the village then I will move, but He hasn't told me that.

Abraham left Ur, and he never went back. A man of God is a servant to everybody, and he does not have a specific home. This is what Jesus explained in Mark 10:29, which explains that we have to do away with the wisdom of the world, which is still holding many bound today even when they claim to be believers.

In Matthew 19:21, Jesus also explained this to the rich young man, to leave all to follow Him. Another verse where Jesus emphasised separation is Luke 9:59-60: *And he said unto another, Follow me. But he said, Lord, suffer me first to go and bury my father. Jesus said unto him, Let the dead bury their dead: but go thou and preach the kingdom of God.*

While I was still wondering why the innocent woman was being accused of something she knew nothing about because she too was trying to adjust to my new life since I answered God's call, I heard a voice: 'you are to write a book on marriage.' That was when I realised that the text message came so that I would have something to write about. Here is the text she sent to my wife, showing how wives are being tormented by ungodly sisters-in-law:

'I thought your coming to our family will be for love, blessing, favour, joy, goodness etc. It became hatred, separation, badness,

CHAPTER TWELVE

sadness, bitterness, failure, disappointment. You need to change, if not, GOD OF (the church) I SERVE WILL VISIT YOU.'

I deleted the name of the church she included so as not to trigger unnecessary reactions. Then she sent another text to my wife which read:

'Outside you are good while inside you Hum! Hum! I say Hum!, Madam you deceive everyone in the world, But you cannot deceive three (3) personalities (1) yourself (2) Satan (3) God Almighty. ...... Be warned, the judgment....'

Well that was the end of this text message.

In all this, she forgot that she was talking to the wife of a servant of God, meaning she had also disregarded me and the anointing upon me, just as happened to Moses. I had earlier received many text messages from her where she would insult me, and close my ears. My father would intervene and that would be it. This time I had to call her, but she wouldn't let me talk, she was just insulting me on the phone.

Now, looking through her text, she made mention of her expectations: love, blessing, favour, joy, goodness etc. What she now sees is hatred, separation, badness, sadness, bitterness, failure and disappointment. To cage herself in the wrath of God she ended up calling God to be the judge.

I am happy that they noticed the separation, because that is what makes me a believer. I remember how Samuel was separated from his family early enough to allow him to mature

CHAPTER TWELVE

in the wisdom of God. Abraham was separated from his family. After Jacob was blessed and Esau got wind of it, he was also separated. All I know is that the God we serve is a God of separation. All she saw befalling her which she now blames on my wife was the evidence of someone dining with the devil. For someone to experience hatred, separation, badness, sadness, bitterness, failure and disappointment shows that there is something wrong which definitely has to do with the devil. It is only the devil who I know will not see joy.

Well, the facts are there for us to see. Many sisters-in-law, as I mentioned earlier, will not mind their homes but will stay to fight their brother's wife. In most cases they would only fight the woman who has stayed with her husband to ensure that he succeeds. I have noticed that for men who don't succeed in life, no sister-in-law torments them.

I will encourage every man to stand with his wife and plan together. If a man will break faith with his wife to please his relatives, then he will be doomed for life. Below is some biblical advice that will help us out.

- Every man must love his wife and not break faith with her, else God will not answer his prayers:

And this have ye done again, covering the altar of the Lord with tears, with weeping, and with crying out, insomuch that he regardeth not the offering any more, or receiveth it with goodwill

CHAPTER TWELVE

at your hand. Yet ye say, Wherefore? Because the Lord hath been witness between thee and the wife of thy youth, against whom thou hast dealt treacherously: yet is she thy companion, and the wife of thy covenant. - Malachi 2:13-14

- Marriage is about separation from the outside. Cleave to your wife. This is what the Bible says:

Therefore shall a man leave his father and his mother, and shall cleave unto his wife: and they shall be one flesh. - Genesis 2:24.

- Every man should love his wife wholeheartedly, because the God we serve will surely support their actions provided they favour the vision of God for the family.

Live joyfully with the wife whom thou lovest all the days of the life of thy vanity, which he hath given thee under the sun, all the days of thy vanity: for that is thy portion in this life, and in thy labour which thou takest under the sun. - Ecclesiastes 9:9.

And God said unto Abraham, Let it not be grievous in thy sight because of the lad, and because of thy bondwoman; in all that Sarah hath said unto thee, hearken unto her voice; for in Isaac shall thy seed be called. - Genesis 21:12

And for the wife, you must try to ensure you keep on building your home, and prayerfully defending it even against your own people, because you have an obligation to fulfil before God in the marriage. Don't allow the attack

CHAPTER TWELVE

from in-laws to deter your love for your husband. See what the Bible advises below:

- No wife should do her husband evil, no matter what.

She will do him (her husband) good and not evil all the days of her life. -Proverbs 31:12.

- Every wife should know that her primary duty is to build her home and defend it against spiritual cobwebs. Wisdom is of God, so meet God to guide you in this adventure. If the man fails, you fail also. And in many African cultures, if the man dies, it is the wife they will lay the blame on. Love your husband. Studies have shown that the rate of men dying from high blood pressure is increasing. Please keep checks on your nagging due to family in-laws pumping up your anger.

Every wise woman buildeth her house: but the foolish plucketh it down with her hands. - Proverbs 14:1

CHAPTER THIRTEEN

THE CASE FOR THE CHURCH

Every church leader should know that marriage is ordained by God and therefore it should be supported with all it takes to ensure it succeeds. They must teach their members about this. I have seen churches where even the pastors have divorced their wives.

Many church practices show that they have mixed doctrinal wisdom with worldly wisdom. Some would ask: 'what would Jesus' response have been if He were to give His opinion about how marriages should be in the 21st century?' My answer is that nothing would have changed. He only came to fulfil the law, and to set the pace for reconciliation with God. This explains the church's involvement in marriage, to reconcile everyone back to their first love – Jesus Christ, the foundation of all things.

Some churches prior to marriage will want the intending couples to perform a pregnancy test. My argument has been, is it the pregnancy that is the problem or that they should stay off sex until they are married? This, however, is a social solution to a spiritually-decaying system. The problems we see in society today points to the fact that the message of Christ hasn't be preached yet. Even in the multitudes of church buildings with hundreds of supposed worshippers, we have paid lip service to the doctrine of repentance and the world is suffering already for it. To the clergy, Ezekiel 34, gazes at your face. It is time to make amends.

I will be discussing the practices of the church which have either helped the institutionalization of marriage or helped to mar it, the institution of which they are supposed to be custodians. Then we will discuss how the church can position itself in order to enable couples to live a worthwhile life, pleasing unto God.

How the church helped to institutionalise marriage

The term 'church' means those called for the service of God. If we accept this definition, then we would say that the first church started when God gave man instruction relating to marriage and sexual acts. That takes us into the Exodus of the Israelites, from the land of Egypt into the wilderness. Here, marriage was institutionalized to prevent immoral acts and for the first time, there was an ordained priestly legal system regulating the practice of marriage, which set it apart from the practices of all other cultures.

The Levitical laws, as seen earlier in chapter 10, established the basic order of what governs the institution

CHAPTER THIRTEEN

today. Then the order of marriage and what goes on after marriage was constituted and could be tenable before the tabernacle of God. In the book of Malachi 2:13-16, God made it known to man that He was indeed a witness to the marriage bond. This clearly places the church at the forefront of the marital union. Again we would see God returning Abraham's wife to him even after Abraham had given her a 'secular divorce,' by denying her in public.

Over the years, marriage laws as practised by the church have greatly varied from what they used to be in the Levitical era in the Bible. This is a result of the infiltration of other cultures and the teachings of Jesus Christ. As the years go by, due to the interaction of humans with their immediate society, the church has approved certain rules and regulations to keep the changes to marriage in check. The Catholic Church, for instance, does not believe in divorce, except in cases of unfaithfulness. The Pentecostal churches have varied views, due to their understanding of their own doctrinal research. They have developed laws in their domains to ensure they are able to regulate the practice of marriage to suit their own doctrinal principles.

There was a time in my village when, for the Anglican church to confirm someone, he had to be seen as the husband of one wife, and if he had more than one wife or concubine outside, he had to divorce or renounce the union before he could be confirmed. This practice is not in the Bible as defined, but could be seen as a regulation intended to bring sanity in marriages. Jehovah's witnesses also do not support divorce as far as I know.

Today, many have come to embrace the participation of the church in their marriages because the church preaches monogamy, and many are also seeing the importance of God in their homes as the reason for the peace they will enjoy over time.

How the church destroys the marriage institution
While the church helped to get the ideals of marriage accepted as a holy institution dedicated to God, it also, in trying to interpret the doctrinal requirements of marriage, injected some ills into it. These include the relegation of the woman to someone who cannot minister in the church. This has made many women see themselves as not important to the affairs that would bring development. And, because they have this nonchalant attitude towards growth and development, occasioned by the church's neglect of their gifts, they have grown to disapprove everything the man does. As such there will be little or no progress in homes where the woman has a perception created by the church that she is only a listener and not one who would offer advice or suggestions.

Another area in which the church has erred is in tithe paying. I see no reason why the husband and the wife would

CHAPTER THIRTEEN

not combine their tithes. Why should they pay separately? This act will continue to breed disunity in homes. As I said earlier, some churches see the conducting of pregnancy tests as a confirmation that marriage can be constituted. This does not stop the intending couple from copulating using protective devices, such as the condom. If we are preaching abstinence, we should hold fast to it.

Many churches have also refused to constitute a marriage where the girl is already pregnant. Where are we sending them out to? Should we refuse to accept those who have come to God in their shame, because of trying to please men? Adam and Eve sinned and God took them and clothed them. We should accept these couples, but tell them the consequences of what they have done, spiritually (dishonouring God) and physically (the possibility of having a child with sickle cell anaemia). The Bible says, in John 6:37: *All that the Father giveth me shall come to me; and him that cometh to me I will in no wise cast out.*

Expensive church weddings are on the increase, but they only leave the newly-wedded hungry and in need. Many ministers see marriage as an avenue for mass evangelism, and encourage their members to invite guests to fill their auditoriums. This is bad and non-doctrinal. Jesus was at the wedding feast, but He never saw it as an event where He would blow His trumpet. Rather he said to His mother, in John 2:4: My *time has not yet come.*

CHAPTER THIRTEEN

These days pastors shout at the tops of their voices so that everyone sees them as miracle workers. After Jesus had turned water into wine, did He shout to let those at the wedding feast know He was a miracle worker? No! The noise in churches these days confirms that they are becoming like the empty vessels which make the loudest noise. In some churches, the process of marrying members is somewhat cumbersome and I have seen these members go to other churches to marry, yet would still come to the church that rejected them to become deacons and deaconesses. Whom are we deceiving? Some churches would not wed intending couples who don't have their own car. Others want to wed only the children of the rich. And, again, until it is time for marriage classes, many young Christians, especially the young, have no idea of what marriage entails, as many church messages are not focusing on this aspect of the Christian foundation. Many young couples are afraid of the marriage process in many of our churches. The rules are too money-oriented. In some churches, the couple must buy a gift for the church before they are attended to.

How the church can help to sustain marriages
Now that we have seen the impact of the church on marriage, especially when it is seen as the arm of God on earth, the church needs to refocus on the drive to return every child of

CHAPTER THIRTEEN

God back to Him. We can achieve this through:

1. Starting marriage training on time. It should be announced that anyone intending to marry within a space of one year should register for a free marriage training session. During this period, they should be introduced to happily-married couples in the church who would act as mentors to ensure that they are learning as the training goes on.

2. The church should work on the doctrinal principle of rejecting all intending couples who had known each other before the wedding day. Rather, the church should be blamed for paying lip service to immoral sexual acts.

3. The church needs to formalise its involvement in the marriage process, from making the choice of partner to the wedding ceremony. The church should lay more emphasis at this stage on upbringing values, so that parents should know that they owe God a duty to properly train their children on the kind of values they must grow with in order to become successful in their marriages.

4. The church should at no time encourage divorce. Rather, acts that would lead to infidelity should be continually preached as against the will of God for mankind, instead of concentrating our messages on financial prosperity because we want to build impressive cathedrals. The reason the church is unable to live to please God is that

CHAPTER THIRTEEN

many pastors think they have become God and do not need to help others see the God in heaven. So the congregation sees him as their God and would worship him, leading many people astray who now operate their lives and their marriages on human wisdom. In most cases this is borne out of the failure the pastor is experiencing in his home. I have seen pastors' wives who dress like whores, and before we know it, the church community becomes a den of whoredom.

5. The church should, after the wedding day, keep on encouraging the newly-wedded to strive on, emphasising to them that the devil hates marriages and that he would stop at nothing until he caused them to divorce. This way, newly-wedded couples will know that they are engaged in spiritual warfare.

6. More marriage seminars should be conducted with focus on the salvation of marriages from satanic wisdom, not a forum to encourage believing mothers to dress half-naked so as to attract their husbands. I am not comfortable inviting a medical doctor to teach my members on how to have sexual fun, yet this is the practice of many churches these days. These practices are even stopping many doctors from repenting and giving their lives to Christ, because they believe that even the pastors have no moral and

CHAPTER THIRTEEN

spiritual justification to advise them to repent when these same pastors use worldly wisdom to train their members on sexual acts.

7. Inviting a lawyer to a couples' dinner so that he can teach couples about the process of seeking divorce if the need arises is satanic, and any church that practises it is doomed to eternal hell. Speak as a prophet sent to tell this generation their sins. The voice of the Lord echoed in my night vision on the 26th of May 2012: *Who will go before me like Moses and Elijah did, to tell this generation their sins so that they would repent?*

8. The church should go back to preaching the old-time message of salvation: 'repent, for the kingdom of God is at hand.' No human wisdom will save our marriages. We must all repent from our evil ways. The broken cistern we hewed for ourselves in the church is draining us dry: *For my people have committed two evils; they have forsaken me the fountain of living waters, and hewed them out cisterns, broken cisterns, that can hold no water* - Jeremiah 2:13.

CHAPTER FOURTEEN

THE CASE FOR SOCIETY

One day my wife called me to help her to get money from the ATM machine with her card. When I got to the machine, I tried the PIN three times and the card was retained by the machine. When I went to the bank to collect the card I had almost become a criminal, and I had to call my wife to the bank. Society and its legal system could also be blamed for the distrust we have in marriages today. They have defined marriage as a contractual agreement, and many marry for what they can get out of it.

Every society has its own traditional cultures and religious practices. The case for the culture, tradition and legal authorities that prevail has to do with the laws in society which regulate marriage. The Nigerian constitution, for instance, sees marriage as a means of national integration:

'For the purpose of promoting national integration, it shall be the duty of the State to: encourage inter-marriage among persons from different places of origin, or of different religious, ethnic or linguistic association or ties' (The Constitution of the Federal Republic of Nigeria, 1999, Chapter II, 15.3c)

CHAPTER FOURTEEN

Our present society sees a marriage as a lateral legal agreement between two people. In most cases they would not say 'male and female'. It is seen as based on the fulfilment of some spelt-out obligations on both parties in the agreement. It is binding on them only as long as each spouse performs their respective duties according to the contract in place. If, however, one spouse fails to adequately uphold the salient terms of the legal document or contract, the other can choose to no longer be bound by the contract. This will only encourage divorce and separation.

This proviso makes each party, man and woman, who wants to get married see the union as a legal entity, which could be dissolved at will. In Africa, and especially in Nigeria, the culture we were born into frowns at wanton divorce, as the culture sees the woman as goods purchased by the man. I have been in a meeting where a man actually referred to his wife as someone he bought.

Our legal systems and concepts are an offshoot of English common law, which sees a marriage between a man and a woman as a contractual and voluntary confidential agreement. As seen in the Bible, English common law also views marriage as the foundation of the family unit and essential in order for the society to preserve moral, traditional and cultural values, and the transfer of same. As also seen in the book of Proverbs 31:10-31, the wife's obligations include

CHAPTER FOURTEEN

the making of the home (Proverbs 14:1), not denying her husband sexual relations and bringing up their children. With changes in our societies, the definition of marriage is changing too, and these deviations are negating the values expected by God in our marriages.

Below are some of the instances of how society has affected the marriage institution, as quoted below:

- In 1996, President Clinton of the United States, signed into law the Defense of Marriage Act (DOMA) (http://thomas.loc.gov/cgi-bin/query/z?c104:H.R.3396:), which, for federal purposes, defined marriage as 'only a legal union between one man and one woman as husband and wife' (1 U.S.C. § 7). DOMA further provided that 'No State, territory, or possession of the United States, or Indian tribe, shall be required to give effect to any public act, record, or judicial proceeding of any other State, territory, possession, or tribe respecting a relationship between persons of the same sex that is treated as a marriage under the laws of such other State, territory, possession, or tribe, or a right or claim arising from such relationship' (28 U.S.C. § 1738C). - http://www.law.cornell.edu/wex/marriage
- All states of the USA limit people to one living husband or wife at a time and will not issue marriage licences to anyone with a living spouse. Once an individual is married,

CHAPTER FOURTEEN

the person must be legally released from the relationship by death, divorce, or annulment before he or she may remarry. Other limitations on individuals include age and close relationship. Limitations that some but not all states prescribe are: the requirements of blood tests, good mental capacity, and being of opposite sex. (http://legal-dictionary.thefreedictionary.com/Legally+married)

I have decided to use the US legal documentation on marriages above because of the rate of single parents, gay marriages, and divorce prevalent in the US, which to me, contravenes God's plan for marriage.

In most African countries, the administration of marriage is still being done in the cultural way. The church also throws its weight behind the institution, and this is the reason why in Nigeria intending new couples often undergo traditional, registry and church marriage as a means of fulfilling the marriage process, although I do not see all these as reasons why the marriage will ever work. For instance, in the same 1999 constitution of the federal republic of Nigeria, second schedule, part I, item 61, under 'exclusive legislative list,' the legislative powers of the state do not extend to the marriages celebrated under Islamic or Customary laws, as quoted inter alia:

'The formation, annulment and dissolution of marriages other than marriages under Islamic law and Customary law including matrimonial causes relating thereto.'

Which means that even if the legal system nullifies the

CHAPTER FOURTEEN

marriage based on the agreement entered before the law at the registry, until it is customarily nullified, that marriage still holds. This fact may have informed the decision of the church to ensure that every marriage is celebrated according to custom before going to the registry to involve the government and then to the church, where they now enter into a spiritual vow to uphold their union in sanctity before God. The church sees the involvement of the government through the marriage registry as a means to uphold the marriage as tenable evidence in court in the case of matrimonial disagreements leading to divorce.

This also explains the involvement of the prevailing legal system in interfering with God's law concerning marriage. Because of fear of disintegration, laws have been put in place to accept everybody the way they are. This is the problem with the society we live in. The book of Jude 1:3 talks of us being united under the auspices of having a common salvation. The more we have divisions in our laws that contravene God's decrees, the more we will keep on bringing pain in our homes.

How society helped to institutionalise marriage
Society helped to institutionalise marriage through the provision of legal systems which define what should be in place to enable a marriage to be legally tenable in court. In some cases, the court have actually helped to settle disputes.

CHAPTER FOURTEEN

The law has also been used to charge people with matrimonial vices. The state ministry of social welfare has helped to curtail the excesses in marriages with respect to the denial of marital rights. Widows have also been helped to recover the properties of their late husbands.

How society destroyed the institution of marriage
Civilization and the integration of varied cultures has undermined God's concern that darkness and light should not come together. Our schooling system, because the law allows freedom of association, has also brought about the infiltration of unhealthy habits in children. In some schools, despite the rules and regulations in place, it is not uncommon to see students dating each other in school.

The working environment is another area where people tend to compare themselves, and when they perceive that other couples are meeting up in their marital obligations despite the work demand there is usually trouble in their homes over the laxity of their own spouse, forgetting that all fingers are not equal. The usual respect for elders is diminishing so that today, people marry anyhow. There is so much unhealthy information in society that everyone tends to live a life of suspicion. Trust is dying daily as a result of stories people hear. The availability of technology has also brought about unhealthy knowledge about sexual issues, and the opportunity for comparison. In most developed cultures and societies, parents have little influence over the lives of their adult children, which is one reason why we have so many single mothers in these cultures.

How society can help to sustain marriages
We all must go back to God. Jude 1:3 talks about a common salvation. The presence of unbelievers in our society will breed evil daily. These evils are seen everywhere today as divorce, pornography, hatred and disagreement. Society should strengthen its laws to prevent unlawful marriages and divorce. We should see marriage as the foundation of every God-fearing nation. This will help the laws relating to marriages to help us to gain a society free of marital vices.

CHAPTER FIFTEEN

THE CASE FOR MONEY

Why have I decided to talk about money? Quarrels over money affect the peace of many marriages. It is no news that couples fight over money as much as they fight about sex, if not more. Many such fights actually happen while they are trying to get money for the marriage ceremony.

I have decided to talk about money simply because many marriages are breaking daily because of its absence, while some are breaking because there is too much of it. Two issues that have centred on all the marriage counselling I have ministered are sex and money. Even when we talk about the involvement of in-laws as a challenge to many marriages, the underlying reason for the complaints is usually money. Sometimes it is funny to see how money has dealt a blow to the happiness of a home. Today both men and women are chasing after it and in most cases they lose their integrity in the process.

Our discussion on how money has affected the marriage institution, positively and negatively, will be based on the wisdom we will be getting from the following scripture verses:

- *Money answereth all things… - Ecclesiastes 10:19.*

- *For the love of money is the root of all evil: which while some coveted after, they have erred from the faith, and pierced themselves through with many sorrows. But thou, O man of God, flee these things; and follow after righteousness, godliness, faith, love, patience, meekness. -1 Timothy 6:10-11*

- *But if any provide not for his own, and especially for those of his own house, he hath denied the faith, and is worse than an infidel. – 1 Timothy 5:8*

Let's take a look at the first verse above. Money solves all problems, is what the preacher seems to be saying in Ecclesiastes 10:19. Is this a metaphorical statement? How can money answer all things? To understand what the preacher meant, we need to look at what led to this statement. Many women have quoted this verse to support their arguments for why their husbands must give them more money, because as they claim, their joy will only come when the man brings in more money, which will automatically answer all things. Many of these women are been deceived by their seemingly corrupt pastors and prophets who want them to sow seeds into their own lives so that these marriages would work. Now that verse referred to opens with: 'A feast is made for laughter, and wine maketh merry.' There are four key words there: feast –

CHAPTER FIFTEEN

celebration, laughter – display of joy in the heart of those celebrating and could also mean the act of mockery; wine – substance of celebration, and finally, merry – the visible effect of wining and dining seen in those involved. The concluding part of that verse refers to all these effects, that money was the reason behind what we just explained. We can say therefore, from what the preacher said, that 'money paves the way for unending celebration.'

Now that we are clear about this verse, we also need to ask ourselves if money will just drop from the sky. No! This explains further the context of the verse above – simply meaning that after work, you should spend time to relax and spend some money on yourself, and since one person cannot have a feast, borrowing a leaf from 1 Timothy 5:8, every home must spend time together to celebrate and enjoy the fruits of their labours.

This means in totality that money would not be there to spend all the time. There are times of high spending, and times of doing without. Feasts are not celebrated every day: *Blow up the trumpet in the new moon, in the time appointed, on our solemn feast day* - Psalms 81:3. Merriment also is not an everyday event, otherwise it would not be mentioned as a special event in the Bible, implying that couples should not wear themselves out trying to have more money to spend. There must be a time to come together and celebrate.

CHAPTER FIFTEEN

This fact will lead us into the next verse quoted earlier, which is 1 Timothy 6:10-11. Now we are told that the love of money can lead us into pain, because no evil occurs without injecting pain into our lives. And it further warned that anyone filled with the spirit of the Lord should desist from loving money. My father once advised me while I was growing up: 'Those who chase after money will some day get chased by money.' As I grew into maturity, I could see that those who chase after money end up having bitterness and sorrows.

An American R&B singer, Millie Jackson, once sang that love is a dangerous game. Love usually involves giving. This means that when we love money too much, we are going to give all our time to it, and we may end up saving money for others while we rot in our graves. The love of money is actually bred during courtship and in most cases men are to be blamed. They tell so many lies while trying to woo the lady. They make so many promises to her, promising her the entire universe. The woman suddenly starts seeing the promises instead of the man standing before her. Years later, when she begins to see that those dreams are becoming fantasies, she will scream for help.

I have found that many women also entice the man into proposing to them through the use of money in providing whatever he needs to be accepted as a man by her parents and friends. I have seen women buy cars, clothes, shoes etc, just to make the young man look decent to his would-be in-laws. A few years later, they discover that they have been living in the euphoria of infatuation and white lies.

The foundation a marriage grows on will determine if it will live up to the expectation of God. Any marriage founded on lies and deceit will only head towards the rocks. Jesus told Pilate that those who hear the truth hear him. This implies that those who speak and hear lies hear the devil, because he is the father of lies – meaning that any marriage existing on lies is the devil's tent. And because the devil moves to and fro, it explains why such a marriage will not experience peace. Couples should make it a point of duty to tell the truth, no matter what. Promoting oneself in order to belong to where we are not presently is sin.

The last verse, 1 Timothy 5:8, linked the inability of the man to provide for his household to an infidel. Does this mean that without money, we cannot run marriages successfully?

Managing money requires wisdom, and the language of successfully managing money is prudence. Many of us have grown the ladder of academic pursuit but have never given a thought to how to make and spend money. When a couple finds it difficult to account for the money they spend, there will be trouble in the home.

What then is prudence? Let's see what the Bible says about it. Prudence in spending means that:

- We must spend wisely – buy only what we need. I would challenge both husbands and wives here. Men often spend

CHAPTER FIFTEEN

money on alcoholic drinks, cigarettes and women. Some believers, though they don't indulge in what I listed earlier, end up spending money on unnecessary electronic devices. Some phones are just too expensive for the kind of income they have. Many married people spend too much on unnecessary journeys. And because we waste money, our days of rest become reduced as we have to work again to fill our pulses. In the developed world, the use of credit cards has also made many couples depend on borrowed money.

- Planning – this is vital to the survival of any marriage. Jesus told us that anyone who wanted to build a house must first count the cost. Many marriages are dying today because of lack of planning.

- Saving – in my book *How good and large is your land?* I proposed that we can save 30% of our monthly income. Why do we save? We save for the future and for our children. The struggle people go through in life, which has become more of an ordeal in the hands of the devil, is because many of us don't know how to save for tomorrow. Every married couple who wants to succeed must endeavour to live on savings, and not on borrowed money.

The Israelites borrowed jewels from their Egyptian neighbours as they proceeds on their wilderness journey. They didn't know the value of what they had borrowed because they

CHAPTER FIFTEEN

hadn't saved to buy them, so they threw them on the fire for Aaron to make a golden calf for them. It is simple reasoning. Of what use would gold and silver mean to people who have being living as slaves?

Those who don't make savings squander whatever comes their way. Show me a husband or wife who wastes money, food, water, etc, and I will show you one who doesn't save for tomorrow.

- Making money – we need to also learn how to use money to make more money. This is what is called investment. Every couple should know how to make more money in a non-stressful manner. When making money takes all our time we become stressful, and this will also affect our days of family get-togethers.

- Accountability – without accountability, there is no prudence. I have seen many women angry over a husband's request to account for the money they spend, and even their salaries. They see that as the man being overbearing. Some men also don't feel their wives should ask them what they spend their money on. Any marriage where both parties are unable to show good accountability for money spent will one day head for the rocks. It is my belief that every man should tell his wife and children how he spends the family money. As the custodian of the family wealth,

CHAPTER FIFTEEN

every man should be responsible enough to show restraint in spending.

- Debt-free living – This is the hallmark of satisfaction. Nothing brings more joy than knowing that the day we die, nobody will come harassing our families over a debt we have left. While many feel it is hard to stay away from debt, I believe it is feasible. My wife and I made a concerted effort to become debt free, and we did so. And the unnecessary high blood pressure I used to have reduced because God gave me the wisdom to stay off debt.

  The debts we take on include loans for school fees because we send our children to expensive schools, car loans, sometimes because we want to belong to a higher group in society, credit card debts as a result of trying to live above our income and debts from gambling, making most believers come to the altar with a financial burden. The fact that one partner has more debt than the other, or one partner is debt free, will often cause quarrels in the home when they sit down to talk about income, spending habits and debt repayment, because the less susceptible partner may feel cheated. The Bible says in Proverbs 22:7: *Just as the rich rule the poor, so the borrower is servant to the lender.*

- Unproductive shopping – some women want to buy anything any time. Unworn clothes are all over the place.

CHAPTER FIFTEEN

Shopping sprees are never a good habit for those desiring success in life. I have worked with women who spend all their earnings on items of low value.

- Reducing bills – making only productive calls will help reduce our phone bills, using only the amount of electricity needed will help us to reduce electricity bills and hospital bills can be reduced by staying healthy rather than eating junk food – meat pies, chicken pies, chocolate, sugar-filled food and so on. We need to remind ourselves that whatever will not add to our savings should be detested. I don't make unproductive phone calls. I know that with every hello I make, the phone companies are smiling to the banks. My phone calls should add value to my life.

In order to pay bills, many homes have what they refer to as Mine, Yours and Ours. This is not the attitude of a family who should live together. The Bible says that they are now one flesh. The reason for this is because both partners work and they seem not to agree on financial issues. In such cases they may decide to split the bills in percentage terms. I have seen homes where the woman will call the husband to demand his percentage of the rent. Once they have each serviced their own portion of the domestic bills, each spouse can spend what they have left as they see fit.

CHAPTER FIFTEEN

This may sound like a logical arrangement, but it often leads to bitterness in the home, as the man may lose his grip on it, thus dividing the home and diminishing the value of the marriage. For women, if you are the one with the cash, be careful how you present certain spending decisions. Every man has his ego and will not trade this out for the sake of love.

- Wasteful cooking – people will eat anything today, at the expense of tomorrow. Some soup products are not healthy to the pocket, containing all the different parts of a cow for instance, mixed with seafoods. In the end many end up throwing this expensive food in the waste bin.

- Frugality for the work of God – while giving to the work of God is a necessity to help His work and spread the gospel of our Lord, many families have been duped over this. Some prophets and pastors see the work of pastoring as a business for climbing the mountain of success in life, and use every opportunity to persuade their members to spend what they could have saved for the future.

- Generous giving – a prudent wife or husband will know when to give generously and when not. We can learn from Abraham. He was rich, yet he had to engage his servants daily for them to earn his generosity. Especially in Nigeria, many people expect those working to keep on giving to

CHAPTER FIFTEEN

them. This is the reason why many homes seem to celebrate ill-gotten wealth. I have seen those who just want to sleep while others could fend for them. Meeting the needs of extended families is one of the reasons for poor marriages in many homes. Help as much as you can. Apply wisdom in your act of generosity.

- Simple living – To live simply means maintaining a low profile in society. Jesus did not live the life of a God who owns the heavens and the earth. His simple life was seen in the night when He was arrested. It was after Judas had kissed Him that they knew He was Jesus. Every couple should live a simple life. Let people see the God in you and not the money in your pocket. We should stop worshipping money so that our living does not depend on it.

- Foolishness management
People need to manage their foolish acts. The reason many marriages are experiencing financial hazards is the husband and wife's inability to make the right decisions. In all, let us take the advice of our Lord to heart:

And why do you worry about clothes? See how the lilies of the field grow. They do not labour or spin. Yet I tell you that not even Solomon in all his splendour was dressed like one of these. If that is how God clothes the grass of the field, which is here today and tomorrow is thrown into the fire, will he not much more clothe you,

CHAPTER FIFTEEN

O you of little faith? So do not worry, saying, 'What shall we eat?' or 'What shall we drink?' or 'What shall we wear?' For the pagans run after all these things, and your heavenly Father knows that you need them. But seek first his kingdom and his righteousness, and all these things will be given to you as well. Therefore do not worry about tomorrow, for tomorrow will worry about itself. Each day has enough trouble of its own. -Matthew 6:28-34 (NIV)

Money-making marriage
Some marriages make money, even enough to give some away, while other couples consume money with little or none to give out. Money comes through appreciation. When we have the wisdom of God in us, people who desire God will definitely desire us because the Lord lives in us, and this will be seen through the attitudes we display. Once we are desired, whatever we do, we will also receive this desire and the admiration of people. This is how increase comes. The more people appreciate what you do, the more the money will flow naturally.

Some believe that it is not morally right for Christians to make money. This is a fallacy. Money-making is the result of the application of wisdom. The only thing we should be careful about is not to apply the wisdom of the world in making money, or we will become poor as a result of the sorrows that we will go through, leading us into the life of shame (Jeremiah 8:9). The blessing of the Lord makes us rich.

CHAPTER FIFTEEN

This blessing is the Holy Spirit, who gives us the right wisdom to live daily, as man is not supposed to live by bread alone (Matthew 4:4). Those who live by bread alone, suddenly become worn out from the chase of money. With wisdom you can achieve more than you ever expected (Ecclesiastes 10:10). Let's see what the Bible says also in Proverbs 3:13,14: *Joyful is the person who finds wisdom, the one who gains understanding. For wisdom is more profitable than silver, and her wages are better than gold.*

Are you looking forward to receiving wages that far outweigh what gold can offer? Then seek wisdom.

A money-making marriage is a marriage that has not yielded to the pressure of living for money, but where the husband and his wife see money as a means to meeting the needs of the family without allowing the absence of it to steal away their joy and peace. For this to happen, the couple must take the following advice to heart:

- Communicate exhaustively – deliberate with biblical principles why some financial spending decisions must not be made. This is the key to solving most marital financial challenges. The husband should never push his weight as the head of the family through this process. His wife must constructively come to terms with him.

- Do not pay too much attention to position, personality and

CHAPTER FIFTEEN

pride - what I often call the 3Ps. The man occupies the position of the head and as such sees himself as the most qualified authority to take decisions on hard financial spending, like buying a house, for instance. And you will find out that his position, personality and pride is the physical display of the ego in the man.

I have met women who just keep quiet, watching their husbands make all the mistakes, with the excuse that the man wouldn't listen to them. I don't agree with this, as the man is seeing his wife as a stooge. Such a man will not succeed with his overbearing decision-making habit for long. In fact such men end up becoming the stooges to their wives.

The 3Ps are an aspect of every relationship that will play a major role in your financial plans and the amount of joy in your marriage. During courtship, this can easily be observed and addressed. Talking about your dreams and aspirations in life during this period of courtship can be of great value, in the sense that it enables you to discover these egotistical elements in each other. This can be played out during the marriage class so that it can be addressed before you move ahead into the marriage. Every couple should know that more than often, marriage is a kind of power play, where the man always wants a 'yes sir' from his

CHAPTER FIFTEEN

wife. This would not be so if not for the sin of Adam and Eve, in Genesis 3:16: *Your desire will be for your husband, and he will rule over you...* But a saved child of God shouldn't even think that marriage is about the show of financial power play. What belongs to the man equally belong to his wife, and vice versa.

- Be godly - The book of Proverbs 10:16: *The earnings of the godly enhance their lives, but evil people squander their money on sin.* Every marriage that lasts must found its finances on godly principles. Don't cheat, steal or tell lies in business. Let your hands be clean. The absence of greed from your savings and business is what takes you to the height of financial freedom.

- Save for your children - There is one reason why we seem to labour as we live and this is because we keep re-inventing the wheel. Our parents in most cases have not secured wealth for us and may have incurred debt for us to pay even after their death. Isaac rode on his father's wealth. The children of Israel had the land of Canaan to inherit. The Bible says in Proverbs 13:22: *Good people leave an inheritance to their grandchildren, but the sinner's wealth passes to the godly.* The second part of this verse takes us to the fear of the Lord. If we can fear God, He will open up His treasure house for us, and we will have enough for our own lives and enough also to store for our children.

CHAPTER FIFTEEN

- Don't be in a hurry - We must learn not to expect profit too early in our business but to plan ahead to see that the business strives. Proverbs 20:21: *An inheritance obtained too early in life is not a blessing in the end.*

- Progress review – knowing what is happening to your investment puts you in charge. Proverbs 27:23, 24, says: *Know the state of your flocks, and put your heart into caring for your herds, for riches don't last forever, and the crown might not be passed to the next generation.* Take time to count your hatched chicks, and see how they are faring, on daily basis. If you sleep, your business also sleeps. The Bible says in Psalm 121:4 that God watches over Israel, His investment, day in day out.

- Every decision counts. Many marriages are in financial decline because there is no accountability in financial decisions. Proverbs 31:16 says: *She goes to inspect a field and buys it; with her earnings she plants a vineyard.* We are obliged to take responsibility for our financial actions, and if we do so, we will not make wrong investment decisions.

The three points to note from the verse just referred to are inspection, ownership and investment. Once we consider the first element, inspection, we will know when to take ownership leading to investment so as to avoid a life of IOU (I Owe You). You should owe only to yourself - when you do

CHAPTER FIFTEEN

that, you become rich. When you owe others, you become poorer by the amount you owe. Don't forget that the verse says that she buys the field with her earnings, not with borrowed money. This is a business founded on a solid rock. God didn't have to borrow Jesus from someone to sacrifice – He gave His only begotten son, meaning that God is not indebted to anyone. Learn from God, and be wise.

- Learn to give. Don't hold back what your heart says you should give. If you hold on to it, the Lord will hold your release also. If you don't open your hands, you can't hold anything with them. This is wisdom. Give to those who are in need as your heart leads you. Do not give your tithe as a gift to the needy. This is where many make mistakes in releasing what is meant for the church to the needy. God wants to bless you, don't take laws into your hand. Give to the poor, give to support the work of God. All these levels of giving have their own rewards – be wise. Proverbs 31:20 says: *She extends a helping hand to the poor and opens her arms to the needy.*

- Don't eat your tithe – the devil has blindfolded many and made them eat their tithe or give it to the poor. Anyone who does that is undoing his/herself. As a wife or husband, encourage the family to pay their tithe as a united household, rather than each of them paying separately.

CHAPTER FIFTEEN

This way we can check the source of the devourer coming into our homes. Tithes open up the floodgate of heavenly blessings upon the congregation. This is one blessing source that does not distinguish a believer from a non-believer. The book of Malachi 3:10 is a popular verse that says that eating tithes is stealing what belongs to God. Anyone who eats spiritual food should also be prepared to manage spiritual upsets in life.

CHAPTER SIXTEEN

PRESENCE MANAGEMENT IN MARRIAGE

There is an aspect of marriage that has faded out of relevance in our marriages. This is what I term 'presence management.' I will explain this term using the Bible.

The Bible talks of Shekinah – meaning the presence of God. The moment Adam and Eve sinned against God, they devalued themselves by using fig leaves to cover themselves, but the presence of God immediately after the incident gave them a more lasting solution. This is what presence management in marriage does. If the husband and wife could presence-manage the home with the gifts God has given to them, there would be no anarchy in our homes.

When we pray in the church, we often seek the presence of God because we know it brings joy, authority, command and correction. Adam left God's presence to serve his punishment, likewise Cain. The children of Israel saw His glory and fainted, begging Moses not to allow them in His presence again. We will use this premise to explain further what presence management can do in a marriage.

CHAPTER SIXTEEN

Earlier, we said there were some features and qualities the husband and wife had individually which attracted them to unite as one inseparable entity. Children also have qualities in them which they display in the presence of their fathers and mothers. The absence of these is often what leads to broken marriages.

We are going to start by singing through a typical song of adoration to God emphasising our hearts' desires. Here the composer sings of what God's presence mean to her, and it is titled: 'In Your Presence'. Words and music by Lynn De Shazo - © 1995 Integrity's Hosanna! Music.

In Your presence
That's where I am strong
In Your presence
O Lord my God
In Your presence
That's where I belong
Seeking Your face
Touching Your grace
In the cleft of the Rock
In Your presence O God

I want to go
Where the rivers

CHAPTER SIXTEEN

Cannot overflow me
Where my feet are
On the rock
I want to hide
Where the blazing
Fire cannot burn me
In Your presence O God

I want to hide
Where the flood of
Evil cannot reach me
Where I'm covered by the blood
I want to be where
The schemes of darkness
Cannot touch me
In Your presence O God

You are my firm foundation
I trust in You all day long
I am Your child
And Your servant
And You are my
Strength and my song
You're my song

CHAPTER SIXTEEN

Seeking Your face
Touching Your grace
In the cleft of the Rock
In Your presence O God
In Your presence

In this song we see passion flowing through the verses, expressing the heart's desire of the composer. That is what the singer expects to see from anyone who comes close, to tie a bond of relationship – someone who will make these desires burn into joy at the end of the day. The presence of God is about relationship. The song captures the earnest desires of a heart yearning for joy. It equally captures the fear of destruction and plea for forgiveness.

The overall theme of the song talks of acceptance. I want us to take a closer look at the lyrics and ask ourselves what we wish to happen now in our marriages so that the fire is there from the very beginning. It is always good to look back at the beginning, and try to inject back all the elements that are missing in our marriages. That way, we will reap the joy of marriage.

A lady once told me that she wanted her husband to lift her up into his arms, but looking at the man, it was obvious that he wouldn't have the strength to do that. The woman outweighed him by some kilos. The problem she was having

CHAPTER SIXTEEN

was her husband's inability to play with her as other men do with their wives, including in this case, lifting her up.

I have seen that what we wish to see is what finally defines the life we live and the amount of joy we bring into it. This is my own personal experience. I went praying one day for God to touch my wife because she seemed not to agree with what I do. She suddenly started nagging, and God spoke to me: 'Go home and love your wife – children often look forward to see their mother come back home with something to eat from the market.' When I got home to meditate on what I received, I realised that for a while I had not given her any gift, so I swung into action and she started beaming. That was the problem. God knew her heart, so He let me know where the shoe was pinching. This is the essence of going to God.

Let's now discuss the elements of presence management in marriage

- **Home presence**

A home is different from a house. A home breeds joy and the desire of togetherness. The very first aspect of presence management is the home. Who manages the home? Let's take a look at what our Bible has to say:
Every wise woman buildeth her house: but the foolish plucketh it down with her hands. -Proverbs 14:1

CHAPTER SIXTEEN

...every man should bear rule in his own house. - Esther 1:22
Wives, submit yourselves unto your own husbands, as unto the Lord. For the husband is the head of the wife, even as Christ is the head of the church: and he is the saviour of the body. Therefore as the church is subject unto Christ, so let the wives be to their own husbands in everything. Husbands, love your wives, even as Christ also loved the church, and gave himself for it. - Ephesians 5:22-25

- The husband

The husband must always be at home in spirit. Even if he travels, his presence must be felt at home. This is often the reason children pick up daddy's picture to show that someone special is not at home. Usually there is less joy because of his absence. We often hear in phone calls: 'I miss you.' Are they really missing you? Or they are only saying that to fill the emptiness in their hearts as a result of the negligence you have shown over the years? Are they trying to tell you what you haven't been taking seriously?

Every man should take the 'I miss you' statement to heart, to ponder over it, and not to increase his egotism and nonchalance, to show that he is, indeed, the heavyweight champion of the home. Be 'home-present', whether you are around physically or not. Let the family sincerely miss you, and not because the pastor encouraged your wife to say it to get you back home. 'Let there be light and there was light', says the Bible. And God further separated the light from the darkness.

CHAPTER SIXTEEN

Work with the advantages in your home. Love your wife and children; they are all you've got. The man should join the wife in teaching the children at home and helping them to do their school homework. Provide for their needs, and depending on how you developed your family, they won't make unnecessary demands if you have done well enough to be home-present. They will value you more than material things, because you will be the all-in-all in their lives.

- The wife

Every woman must see herself as the foundation of the home. Let's look at it this way; the man comes into her in an act the Bible sees as 'knowing', and during the process of that knowing the woman can see the heart of the man in her hands as he responds to every instruction given to him, with his eyes displaying his passion towards her and his heart beating in ecstasy, showing that she is indeed in control. And the children grow in her and come out through her. Her husband ejaculates into her, helplessly, as if saying: 'this is me and all I have got, please accept me,' and the children suck her breasts and play with them as if saying: 'without you I am dead.'

This shows that the woman is naturally in charge. This is an honour the woman has in built in her, that no one can take from her. She is in charge, and the Bible passage referred to earlier says that the only way a woman could lose this honour is through acts of foolishness, the making of unwise decisions. The book of Mark 7:21 see foolishness as one of those things that pollute our hearts.

My advice would be that the woman should always seek the wisdom to run her home from God. Our wives and mothers would do better in their home-presence role if they go back to God, seeking His face and asking Him to give them the wisdom, knowledge and understanding that will enable them to effectively manage their homes. I see many going to pray for God to change their husbands to listen to them, and often deny their husbands sex as a means of getting his attention, which in most cases is a fruitless exercise. Any time we meet with God, He will give us the instructions to carry out, so that peace returns to our homes.

- **Integrity presence**

What is integrity? During courtship, we promised ourselves so much. Both husband and wife remember daily the promises they made. When these promises are compared with the current realities, and there seems to be a mismatch, there is going to be grumbling. Let's keep to our marital vows. Honesty should rule our hearts. Lies punch holes in our hearts. We maintain our presence in our homes by fulfilling our promises to each other.

- **Spiritual presence**

This is where many homes have failed. There is no presence

CHAPTER SIXTEEN

of God. This is the primary responsibility of the man. God talked of Abraham thus: *For I know him, that he will command his children and his household after him, and they shall keep the way of the Lord, to do justice and judgment; that the Lord may bring upon Abraham that which he hath spoken of him.* - Genesis 18:19.

Every man must defend his home from the attack of spiritual cobwebs, through taking the lead to submit his family under the guidance of God. I expect every man to be a teacher of the word of God, which fills him with God's wisdom. He should be responsible enough to ensure the family have days of fasting and waiting on the Lord.

- **Authority presence**

I am careful in talking about authority presence because of the controlling factors behind who exercises what authority. These factors include financial power, intelligence power, beauty power, oratory power, spiritual power and so on, which many have used negatively. These powers are suppose to help us foster unity in our homes so that our physical presence will generally bring these strengths of ours to play, in solving problems at home. But we will seldom see that a beautiful woman wouldn't want to be instructed by her husband as queen Vashti did in the book of Esther, which led to her losing her home, and to the eventual downfall of the kingdom of her husband, as the entrance of Esther into the home gave victory to the Jews who were once the labour pride of the kingdom.

CHAPTER SIXTEEN

On the seventh day, when the heart of the king was merry with wine, he commanded Mehuman, Biztha, Harbona, Bigtha, and Abagtha, Zethar, and Carcas, the seven chamberlains that served in the presence of Ahasuerus the king, To bring Vashti the queen before the king with the crown royal, to shew the people and the princes her beauty: for she was fair to look on. But the queen Vashti refused to come at the king's commandment by his chamberlains: therefore was the king very wroth, and his anger burned in him. Esther 1:10-12.

I know many believers will frown at my statement here, because they see it as the arm of God, but we are discussing marriage, and what makes marriage is how both the husband and the wife help to sustain their position and investments. We should not use the gifts in our lives to divide our homes, rather let these authorities help us to find solutions to problems affecting us so that we can grow into relevance.

- **Sexual presence**

Inasmuch as sex enhances the bond of marriage, it is not the reason for marriage, as many would think. If it were, then the act wouldn't fade away a few minutes after it is carried out. What takes centre stage of our thought system all day long? We think of achieving something for the day and then for the future. Sex is like a given – it is always there. This does not imply that many marriages have not shattered because of the inability of one to satisfy the sexual urge of the other.

CHAPTER SIXTEEN

Let there be sexual presence in your homes. Some couples draw up a timetable and both ensure that when the time comes, neither denies the other. There should also a period of spontaneous sex coming out of the show of love, maybe after presenting a gift. Spontaneous sex is heart-filling, as it sends stars of emotional display into our hearts, making both partners yearn for more care in each other's arms. All of a sudden, tears flow – and apologies are often rendered, spontaneously.

I have heard many complain that their wife or husband is too methodical in approaching sex. One claimed that there was usually a long prayer said before the act would start and that during that period, their libido faded. This does not create the 'spontaneous excitement' effect that libido leads to. This is the reason for many women not climaxing into orgasm during sexual intercourse. Many men only try to please themselves, and once they ejaculate they would leave the woman there to groan and moan her fate. The woman does not come quickly, so every man must learn to be patient. The time for sex should not be the time to answer phone calls. Both of you have to be there in body, soul and spirit.

Sex is often highly possessive in that it takes the centre stage of your thoughts. It releases hormones into our bloodstream which often bring calmness in us immediately after the act, and many go to sleep afterwards, although the

CHAPTER SIXTEEN

woman is still wanting more in order to get to her climax. The use of masturbation is increasing, and this affects sexual urge and desire between husbands and wives.

Understand yourselves and know what both of you appreciate about yourselves. A woman once told me that she enjoys her husband trying to have sex without her consent, because it makes her feel that she is still loved, while another will want it negotiated through foreplay. People are different. In all, be present sexually, and your home will experience the presence of joy, peace and tranquillity.

CHAPTER SEVENTEEN

THE CASE FOR SPIRITUAL MARRIAGES

The reason why many marriages are not working is that many men and women are in a spiritual marriage bond. This is very common in Africa, where one hears of such things as spiritual marriage. Women often say that they are married to demons. Neglecting this claim would mean neglecting the spiritual aspect of marriage.

- **Reptilian spiritual husbands**

Many women have sex with reptilian creatures. These are in fact demons. The creature ravages them through their sex organs. Such a woman hates her husband's sexual advances and will ensure there is a quarrel every night before going to bed so that she can sleep separately, undisturbed. I would advise every man to help such a woman out by making sure there is family Bible study and prayers before going to bed. He should also ensure that he is sexually present in the home. Many women behave like snakes on bed, twisting around with piercing tongues as snakes do.

CHAPTER SEVENTEEN

- **Wizards**

The wizard comes into the room where the woman is sleeping without opening the door. He blows into the eyes of the woman, who then goes into a deep sleep, and would have sex with her. Sometimes the woman will feel he is her husband. When this happens continually, she no longer has a sexual urge. One woman actually confessed that she was shocked when her husband told her he was not responsible for the entire sexual encounter she claimed during a hot argument over the husband's demand for sex. She said it had been going on for months.

While growing up in the village, many youths went to witch doctors, who initiated them into the act called 'Ofuovo Jalo Oweze', meaning deep sleep. Many young boys had sex with their mothers or sisters first to activate the demonic spirit, and would confess as they were about to die. This act is still much practised among young men who are naive towards young girls, and in a bid to satisfy their sexual urge they would meet witch doctors to prepare a charm that would make them move about in the night and have sex with women and young girls. Many so-called prophets today, who are evil, are having this act with women, apart from the physical ones they deceive women into. This act is very real and many unbelieving wives are been harassed sexually by these evil people. Though they find it difficult to divulge, they are groaning in pain.

CHAPTER SEVENTEEN

Every woman must yield to God so as to become free from their manipulation. Praying before sleeping will help a lot. A woman having such an encounter can get a bottle of water, raise it towards heaven and pray 'God fill this water with your spirit'. She should then sprinkle the water all over the room where she sleeps to end the evil encounters.

- **Lesbianism and masturbation**

The act of lesbianism is spiritually controlled. These acts kill interest in the real sexual act. No home where the man engages in masturbation will know peace, because the devil is right there taking control of the home. Likewise, a lesbian wife will never allow the home to experience the favour of God. A mother once confessed that she was having lesbian sex with her own daughter – is this not evil enough? These acts are confirmation of spiritual marriages. Some pastors sees them as mere habit, but any habit that will not glorify God is satanic and evil. And every evil is sin. Such must be resisted.

- **Mermaid spiritual wives**

This is prevalent in coastal cities where men have sex with women in their dreams. Such men usually have wet dreams. The sexual act starts with a woman the man knows physically, and then before he knows it he is already having sex, only to see that in reality he is wet.

CHAPTER SEVENTEEN

Anyone who has been into this act or has been harassed by these evil creatures should seek deliverance through confessing before God and prayerfully resisting it.

CHAPTER EIGHTEEN

MANAGING MARITAL VIOLENCE

Any marriage built on a wrong foundation will breed violence. Forensic examination of spouses who died after being attacked by their husbands would dumbfound anyone as to why anyone would murder his/her spouse so brutally.

Marital violence is the result of long-held hatred in the home. This is all the more reason why marriages should be constituted on the principle of love and not infatuation. Many young people confuse infatuation with love. Parents have much to do in the spouse selection process by ensuring they have inculcated the right values in their children. Marriage principles and process should be thought through early enough. With the increasing rate of marital violence and divorce, it calls for concern that all hands must be on deck. My candid advice would be that when couples are not agreeing any more, they should submit their home to the hands of God. Then they should be ready to learn under the mentorship of a couple who enjoy marital bliss, and have done so for about 20 years, with the evidence seen all around them: lovely children, a peaceful home, fear of the Lord, and dedicated to the work of evangelism.

CHAPTER EIGHTEEN

In a home experiencing violence that could lead to a death, the victimised spouse should tell the police, even if it seems they have agreed. This will put the other spouse in check. Many people no longer regard God, and would rather not want their pastor to be aware of such violence in their homes. One couple fought in my office right in front of me, and later I received a text message from the woman insulting me because I had told her it was unhealthy for her to have abandoned her young baby in the hands of someone else to wean.

Another solution is temporary separation, in which case the woman or the man would stay away from home for some time while their pastors and parents ensure they are settled, and brought back into the house of God and prayed for. This is because staying continuously in a home where the couple fights will definitely lead to more attacks.

Matrimonial violence in many cases is a result of drug addiction and if this is dealt with, it could bring peace.

Much marital violence occurs in homes where the couples cohabit and there is no legal marriage in place. Such a union is already constituted by both parties in sin. If such is the case, then both of them should be encouraged to present themselves before God and let the marriage be constituted by the church with the parents of both parties in attendance to witness and give their consent.

Women should know that the rites of marriage are to safeguard them, and they should not see the church as been

CHAPTER EIGHTEEN

unnecessarily demanding when they are meant to go through the process of marriage defined by the church. If, however, one of them becomes a believer while the other does not, and there is no peace in the home, I would refer us to 1 Corinthians 7: 13,15: she is not under any obligation to remain in such a home, and is free to remarry provided the man has said he is no longer interested in the marriage.

Marital violence is the result of a marriage not constituted with the fear of the Lord at heart.

I will advise the following stages as a means to manage marital violence. Once one stage stops the violence, there is no need to continue, but to enjoy the joy and peace that comes with the solution proffered.

- Talk it over. Be open and discuss like friends.
- Bring in your children to mediate if there is still disagreement, not to blame dad or mum, but to play a neutral role in the settlement.
- If the violence is life-threatening, involve the police. You may also want to report it to the state welfare family service.
- If it is not life threatening, talk to your pastor if the other spouse respects God, so that he/she could be called for discussion.
- Talk to the families of both parties if their consent was sought during the marriage process.

CHAPTER EIGHTEEN

- Talk to an NGO involved in settling marital violence for their counselling and advice.
- Talk to a lawyer who specialises in handling marital issues. This may take you to court. Try to secure peace, even while you are in court.
- You may need to temporarily separate at this point, and stay away from him/her. Who knows, this may make your spouse to start missing you.
- During your separation period, seek the face of God for his intervention. Do not engage in any sexual sin – infidelity, lesbianism, masturbation, oral sex, etc, as this will turn the face of God away from you.
- Communicate occasionally by phone, when you feel it is safe to do so. You may invite him/her to a dinner in a family friend's home.
- Exhaust all avenues to seek peace. Don't give up. Pray, pray, pray and continuously pray.

CHAPTER NINETEEN

ENJOYING MARRIAGE AS THE YEARS PASS

Marriage is what you make it, just like a brand new computer which only runs on the operating system that is installed on the hard disk. This installation is done by the man. It is the kind of music you started the party with that tells the guests what dance steps to do. 'The way you dress your bed so you will lie on it', so the saying goes.

Many women leave their husbands and start staying with their children as the years pass. Men who don't have anything to do after retirement may seem bored, and would pick a quarrel with their wives. They may start spending time in the village. To overcome this boredom both husband and wife should plan their retirement to give themselves something to keep them busy.

Here we go back to the chapter where we discussed why men and women marry. If we want our marriages to be sustained, we have to also know that necessity is the mother of invention. As the years go by and we mature, many of us become frail in our emotions and desires since the promises

CHAPTER NINETEEN

we made to each other on the wedding day might not have been fulfilled. This is because we had allowed ourselves to be overtaken by events, and may have not learned from other marriages that we were privy to have heard or witness the reason for their break-up.

I know marriages are meant to last and be enjoyed because I have proof in the Bible. Noah and his family entered into the Ark when he was 600 years old (Genesis 7:6-7). Don't forget that his sons, their wives and his grandchildren were with him, implying that there was indeed a blissful home, and they all lived to obey God, which was the reason why they were saved.

Abraham was 99 years of age when he instructed his wife to prepare a meal for the angels that came to destroy Sodom and Gomorrah. Then she was already 90, yet she obeyed her husband, showing that there was love in the home. Don't also forget that Hagar had given birth to Ishmael, which was supposed to be something that would have made Sarah tell Abraham to go and instruct Hagar, the mother of her son, if she was to act as many women would these days. Moses married at the age of 40, and stayed with his in-laws, rearing his animals for another 40 years before God called him. At the age of 80, he and his family were prepared to go down to Egypt to carry out God's command. Along the way, Zipporah had to save her husband's life.

CHAPTER NINETEEN

In those days, marriages were valued to the extent that even at death, the man and his wife were buried side by side, and this was another source of unity for their children. If these families enjoyed marriage even to such an old age, why can't this generation stay in marriage?

One thing is common in the stories referred above; they all were obedient and God-fearing, implying that the reason why marriages are breaking these days is the absence of God.

In the discussion that follows, we will also see how we can encourage ourselves to stay together through the odds of life.

- **The beauty of tolerance**

Anytime I think of the beauty of tolerance, I remember what Jesus says in Luke 21:19: *In your patience possess ye your souls.* Marriage is about soul tying. In Psalms 23:3, David says *He restoreth my soul.* How does this all play together? From Jesus' statement, we would see that to possess means to be in control of whatever happens in our lives. If you are not the tolerant type, there is no way you can be in control. And from David's statement we would see that to be in control is to surrender under the leadership of God. This takes us to the next fact, found in the last part of Psalms 23:3: *He leadeth me in the paths of righteousness for his name's sake.* Which means the only way to restore the soul of our marriage is to allow God to take us through a path of glory, because we had submitted under His leading through the vows of marriage we made in His altar.

CHAPTER NINETEEN

To fully understand what we should be doing while we are tolerating the odds that come into our marriages, let's see the facts in 2 Chronicles 7:14: *If My people who are called by My name will humble themselves, and pray and seek My face, and turn from their wicked ways, then I will hear from heaven, and will forgive their sin and heal their land.* This implies that sick marriages can be healed by God, which would mean the land referred to above, provided the couples know God, humble themselves, pray and seek the face of God continually through daily family devotions, fasting and praying together, and abhor every element of wickedness. This is the beauty of tolerance, because you are expectant of a fruitful harvest of peace and joy as you grow in marriage.

- **Working with the advantages**

This is one of my favourite pieces of wisdom. Working with the advantages you see helps you to become more focused in life, and you will discover that your complaints will become so few that you may hardly give room to them to start disrupting your life. As the years goes by, rediscover yourselves and see the good sides only. Give less attention to the ugly side of each other's life. The more you do this, the more you will discover that both of you will start adjusting to concentrate on the advantages you now see flourishing in your lives.

My reference for this wisdom is Genesis 1:1-3, where God had

CHAPTER NINETEEN

to separate the light from the darkness, and in that light He invested His creative intelligence. All of us have disadvantages owing to the fact that we lived and had experiences outside the presence of God before we repented. These ugly encounters would not just die off overnight. This is a fact that we must take to heart. If we do this, we will not cry so much over spilled milk but surrender to God, who will finish the work of transformation in our lives so that we become jewels of glory in His hands. Accept yourself on the basis of the realities you see daily. Increase your love for each other by the day, holding each other's hands as you walk down life's unending paths of learning. Occasionally come together, just the two of you, to see the beauty you have added to yourselves because of your relationship. It is lovely to know that without each other's advice you wouldn't have been where you are now. I will advise this: be there when your partner is there. Anything outside this will create room for fault-finding. Always wear each other's shoes, in thoughts and emotional feelings, to know how they pinch.

- **Find joy**

Writing Christian books, playing the piano and music programming gives me joy. Studying the Bible and counselling gives my wife joy. This is what we will do as we grow old in our marriage. Both of us have discovered where our joy lies. All we need to do now is to strengthen this joy

CHAPTER NINETEEN

the more by encouraging ourselves. Sometimes she would stay with me through the night, reading the manuscripts of my books. She joins me to sing while I play the piano, and also help to restructure the song so that it would flow better, using her choir skills. She is happy seeing that young women are happy in marriage. I am surprised sometimes when she tells me of her encounter with some young ladies and how they are responding to the advice she gave to them, and how they would come back to thank God that she counselled them.

A few years back, we used to fight and argue a lot. This is the beauty of knowing the Lord. I know that God will not let you live in pain if you tell Him to help you discover your joy today.

- **Don't overwork yourself**

This is why we must save for a rainy day. As the year grows, you should limit the stress you go through to make money. If you have raised a God-fearing family, this is the time to relax and enjoy. A good pension plan will help you out here. Having few children will enable you to live healthily as you grow old. I have often seen that marriages hardly survive stress, especially as you grow old. We should pray not to experience ill health after the age of 60. If we have this thought in our hearts, we will stop every form of evil we do to ourselves. All the things we do await us after the age of 60.

I have met old people who told me that growing old is not an easy experience because it is a time for sober reflection on

CHAPTER NINETEEN

the kind of life we have lived. It is a time for confession, and regrets for those who have practised evil. If we want to enjoy our marriage till death do us part, in old age, then we should repent of everything that God does not approve of – infidelity, lies, hatred, cheating, stealing, deceit, kidnapping, etc. These are the acts we engage in which make us overwork ourselves while we are still young.

CHAPTER TWENTY

THE PRACTICES OF DIVORCE

Divorce is defined as 'the legal dissolution of the marriage.' This leaves us with the spiritual aspect of the dissolution. Will this ever happen, knowing that the sexual relationship that had occurred had tied both souls together?

God hates divorce (Malachi 2:16) and society in most cases frowns upon it also. If God loved divorce, there is no way He would have sent His only begotten son to die for our sins (John 3:16). God loves forgiveness and this would be seen in the Lord's Prayer. We don't support divorce in our church. This is why anyone going into marriage must be ready to exhaust all avenues to confirm that the woman or man is the right choice.

I don't support people marrying from emotion because this is not the only aspect that makes up marriage. So many women have complained that they married their husbands because they had pitied them due to the continuous request from them for marriage despite their negative response.

CHAPTER TWENTY

Divorce rate

The information I got from a divorce website (http://www.divorcerate.org) shows that most marriages fail, all over the world. This is one of Satan's weapons to bring people out of God's kingdom. Forgiveness is the key in the kingdom of God. Divorce can only happen when there is no forgiveness. This alarming figure is enough for everyone with the fear of God to return to Him so that peace may once again reign in our marriages.

Causes of divorce
- Lack of effective communication between spouses.
- Lack of sexual satisfaction.
- Childless marriage.
- Trouble from in-laws.
- Lack of knowledge about the purpose of marriage.
- Absence of God in the home.
- Male child syndrome.
- Poor financial support from the man.
- Infidelity on both parts, but mostly on the part of the woman as many women tolerate their husband's immoral acts.
- When trust disappears.
- Family background – poor upbringing, raised by nagging parents.
- Couples who grew up with separated couples.

CHAPTER TWENTY

- Remarried couples.
- Couples having been born out of marriage.
- Cohabitating.

Effects of divorce

Every divorce comes with a negative impact on the spiritual, social, emotional, financial, and physical wellbeing of the couple affected, and this effect may last for years. Some recover from the instant shock it creates and the battered emotions that result, while others may never get themselves together again. The woman is treated in many circles as a 'Belgium' or 'tokunbo,' which is a derogatory name in Nigeria for a second-hand vehicle. She is seen as having brought shame to her parents.

I have also found out that, regardless of age, many children of divorced parents never overcome the adverse effects of the disruption to the peace that once existed in their homes. The psychological trauma that divorce creates is not worth experiencing.

Unfolding Satan's game plan

Satan's game plan is to mutilate whatever institution God has ordained from the foundation of the Earth. The Bible says: *What therefore God has joined together, let no man put asunder.* Divorce is not of God and therefore every couple must resist the devil's advice to terminate the joy of the Lord in the family.

The Bible also says: *Thou hast been in Eden the garden of*

CHAPTER TWENTY

God; every precious stone was thy covering... - Ezekiel 28:13. What did the devil go there to do? We all know the story of man's fall. He went there to disrupt the peace in Adam's family by sowing discord in the heart of Eve, which made her disregard her husband's explanation concerning the tree in the middle of the garden. The fact that Adam blamed her for the sinful acts they carried out shows that there was divorce brewing already. If it were now, with the curse that Adam incurred, he would have thought of living without her. This is the devil's game plan. We must resist him in our lives today. No more listening to bad counsel. Every counsel of Ahitophel against your marriage has failed this moment in Jesus name! Amen.

How to prevent divorce
- Communicate often. And we should not forget that communication is a two-way process – transmit and receive. We should air our views with love and tenderness. Though a spouse may be angry, it is said that two people cannot be mad at the same time. The other partner should be calm whenever the other is angry, and this way we would not be creating a scene similar to those in the marketplace.

- Looking unto Jesus. To look unto Jesus means that we should be ready to endure the pains that come into our marriage. Adam and Eve were ashamed, but God clothed them at the end of the day. Your spouse may have done something silly, but don't hate him, despise the shame he/she has brought to the family, and move ahead with your life. Don't forget that nobody is perfect. We are all trying to walk this path to righteousness. Help him/her to overcome any form of addiction he/she is into – unfaithfulness, drunkenness, smoking, use of hard drugs, etc, by always pointing your spouse to Jesus, daily.

- Parental training. This is the foundation of life. Every parent should live as examples before their children so that their children do not grow up to hate marriage. Fighting, quarrelling, arguing, insulting one another etc, are all traits that children pick as they grow, and these experiences cloud their memory and would make them have an unsuccessful marriage.

- Not depending on society's values – children, sexual satisfaction, money - but on the value system preached by the Bible.

- Avoiding premarital sex. This reduces the interference caused by comparison between the sex in marriage and that outside marriage. Many couples who complain of sexual dissatisfaction base their complaints on a comparison with their earlier encounters prior to marriage.

- Yielding to God. With God all things are possible. The

more we learn of God, the more we will have more wisdom to live happily in marriage.

- Raising children together. Children come with boundless joy in their hearts. When we raise our children together, there is less likelihood that we will have grudges against each other. Many broken homes are homes where the man is too busy to see what the children would become, and in some homes the mother is too busy chasing after a career.

- Working on our pride. Forgiveness is from the heart, and pride deprives us of the ability to forgive others. No proud person is humble, and without humility, there is no way we would submit for correction.

Where to find help when divorce faces you

- Study the Bible so as to understand the word of God concerning marriage.

- Read marriage-related books like this one, and prayerfully tell God to open up your understanding. It is good to start reading such books before there is chaos in your home. Get one also for your spouse. Words read into the spirit have the power to mar or make your life. This is why you must be careful what sort of books your spouse reads.

- Visit a marriage counselling centre. Maybe your pastor will do well, but be careful, the title of pastor does not qualify

CHAPTER TWENTY

him as one with the wisdom to help you out of your predicament. Many marriages have broken today because of pastors' advice. Others have ended because of fake prophets' soothsaying.

- Talk to a Christian NGO set up as a calling by God to address marital vices. These become what many would call ministries. You will see the hand of God the moment you are counselled.

- Locate a marriage mentor who has enjoyed long lasting peace in his or her marriage.

CHAPTER TWENTY ONE

WIDOWHOOD

Before we consider widowhood, I want to take a look at what every husband or wife should do while they are still alive, and this has to do with the writing of wills. A will is a legal declaration by which a person, also known as the testator, names one or more persons, the executor/s, to manage their estate and provides for the transfer of their property at death to chosen beneficiaries.

Who will be your executor? This is the question that runs in the minds of many men and women. It suddenly becomes so real in their heart that they no longer trust their spouse. As for women, they argue that their husband would marry another wife and spend their wealth on her, which would not have been possible if there was a marriage in place. The men also argue that the woman will spend their wealth on her own family and her new husband, and as such they would want their own brother or a family member to execute their will. Others would want their lawyers to do it, or a close friend whom they trust.

CHAPTER TWENTY ONE

The execution of a will or the absence of one has rendered many children and widows homeless and suffering.

Since I don't believe that a woman should have a separate account or property from that of her husband because both of them are one, I would advise that the choice of who executes the man's will should be in the following order:

- Your wife and children (where the children are adults).

- Your trusted friend, if you do not trust your wife. But your will should will everything to her and the children, except in cases where you have to recognise someone else of importance in your life. In such a case, your wife must be privy to it. Also don't forget that getting your trusted friend to execute your will may automatically mean that he will use that as an opportunity to start sleeping with your wife – and the children will end up suffering, even if that was what you were trying to protect. This takes us back to the fact that you must build your marriage on trust and love.

- Your church, when the two options above fail to meet your expectation - except for churches where the pastor and elders have greedy tendencies, which will be evident in the way funds are managed in the church. In such churches, don't be surprised when the pastor starts making advances to your wife in order to get her consent to waste your wealth. This again takes you back to the fact that you need

CHAPTER TWENTY ONE

to trust and love your wife while you live. She is your best executor, because both of you are one.

In all, no other person can execute your will as your spouse, because at the end of the day, your trusted executors will end up being those who will waste your wealth if that is what you fear.

Now that we have talked about the issue of wills, Let's take a look at how the widow can cope with life after the death of her husband.

The widow

The following are instances of widows in the Bible. I will be recounting the Biblical stories that explain how they coped in their situation and then advise what a widow should do in the face of challenges.

- Anna – She was a widow for 84 years, and her joy came from the service of the Lord: *And there was one Anna, a prophetess, the daughter of Phanuel, of the tribe of Aser: she was of a great age, and had lived with an husband seven years from her virginity; And she was a widow of about fourscore and four years, which departed not from the temple, but served God with fastings and prayers night and day.* - Luke 2:36-37

- The widow who gave a farthing – Jesus appreciated her heartfelt offering, which also explains that she held God in high esteem with her heart, by giving all her living to

CHAPTER TWENTY ONE

God, which would be the only reason Jesus would value her sacrificial offering at that moment when the whole of Israel had gone astray and could not recognise Him as the promised messiah: *And there came a certain poor widow, and she threw in two mites, which make a farthing. And he called unto him his disciples, and saith unto them, Verily I say unto you, That this poor widow hath cast more in, than all they which have cast into the treasury: For all they did cast in of their abundance; but she of her want did cast in all that she had, even all her living.* – Mark 12:42-44

- Elijah's widow – Her willingness to give Elijah the last morsel of bread meant for her and her child demonstrates that she feared God and revered Him. This was how she got the joy to stay in her state: *And the word of the Lord came unto him, saying, Arise, get thee to Zarephath, which belongeth to Zidon, and dwell there: behold, I have commanded a widow woman there to sustain thee. So he arose and went to Zarephath. And when he came to the gate of the city, behold, the widow woman was there gathering of sticks: and he called to her, and said, Fetch me, I pray thee, a little water in a vessel, that I may drink. And as she was going to fetch it, he called to her, and said, Bring me, I pray thee, a morsel of bread in thine hand. And she said, As the Lord thy God liveth, I have not a cake, but an handful of meal in a barrel, and a little oil in a cruse: and, behold, I am gathering two sticks, that I may go in*

CHAPTER TWENTY ONE

and dress it for me and my son, that we may eat it, and die. And Elijah said unto her, Fear not; go and do as thou hast said: but make me thereof a little cake first, and bring it unto me, and after make for thee and for thy son. For thus saith the Lord God of Israel, The barrel of meal shall not waste, neither shall the cruse of oil fail, until the day that the Lord sendeth rain upon the earth. And she went and did according to the saying of Elijah: and she, and he, and her house, did eat many days. -1 Kings 17:8-15

- Elisha's widow – Her faith in what the man of God instructed her to do also show how her hope was pointed towards God: *Now there cried a certain woman of the wives of the sons of the prophets unto Elisha, saying, Thy servant my husband is dead; and thou knowest that thy servant did fear the Lord: and the creditor is come to take unto him my two sons to be bondmen. And Elisha said unto her, What shall I do for thee? tell me, what hast thou in the house? And she said, Thine handmaid hath not any thing in the house, save a pot of oil. Then he said, Go, borrow thee vessels abroad of all thy neighbours, even empty vessels; borrow not a few. And when thou art come in, thou shalt shut the door upon thee and upon thy sons, and shalt pour out into all those vessels, and thou shalt set aside that which is full. So she went from him, and shut the door upon her and upon her sons, who brought the vessels to her; and she poured out. And it came to pass, when the vessels were full, that she said unto her son, Bring me yet a vessel. And*

CHAPTER TWENTY ONE

he said unto her, There is not a vessel more. And the oil stayed. Then she came and told the man of God. And he said, Go, sell the oil, and pay thy debt, and live thou and thy children of the rest. - 2 Kings 4:1-7

The consolation I want every widow to take from these is that if they give their hearts to God, He will sustain them. God is a God of the widows. He feeds them when they are in His plan. Consequently, every widow must be ready to give her time and resources to Him.

A widow in our church was in financial need for a business. When she came, the word of the Lord came that she should cook for me to eat. I informed her and she quickly got the food ready. Since that day, funds have come by surprise to her. She lives in an apartment she paid for with the proceeds she got from the business and she bought a car and brought it one morning for me to dedicate to God. Her help came the moment she released for God's servant. Every widow should however watch this kind of request as many have being duped thereafter. So we can conclude that the only way a widow will stay happy is her relationship with God.

From these premises we would be explaining some issues addressed in the Bible relating to widows.

Care for widows
In the Old Testament, there was no legal provision as far as the Mosaic Law was concerned for the upkeep of widows.

CHAPTER TWENTY ONE

They were the burden of relations, and more especially of the eldest son. Tradition sees it as his responsibility to cater for her from the extra share of the property of his father, and as such it was an imposed responsibility upon him. This responsibility includes also giving them a part of the tithes of their third year increase (Deuteronomy 14:29; 26:12). The widows also benefit from the grain sheaves that were forgotten in the field (Deuteronomy 24:19-21). During religious feasts they also get special attention (Deuteronomy 16:11, 14). But today, my advice would be that the widow should engage herself with a job, which she must have been doing while the husband was alive, or a business the family may have been running together. And with special planning and the fear of the God in her heart, her service of humility and love for God will bring joy to her heart, and she will not even remember she is a widow. Every church should have a special welfare program to care for widows.

Remarriage of widows
St Paul counselled younger widows to remarry (1 Timothy 5:14). What danger does this bring to play when the church, according to the word of God, is preaching monogamy, and many young women who are tired of their marriage would want the man dead so that they can be free to marry another man of their choice? What happens to the children when they remarry? Will she be ready to drive the vision her dead husband left behind?

CHAPTER TWENTY ONE

If we see marriage as a replication of the relationship between the Church and Christ, we would see that Christ expects the Church to carry on with the vision of soul-winning which He lived and died for. Many a woman has vowed not to remarry but to live to see that the vision she once shared with her husband lives on and to see that the children live to appreciate this vision as the years goes by. The only way a woman can live without remarrying is through her ability to burn the fire of righteousness.

I will advise that the younger ones referred to here are those who do not have children yet, and below the age of 60, as mentioned by Paul in the verse referred above, and if they are not soaked in Christ, may decide to remarry. But if Christ would say in Matthew 19:12 that some have made themselves eunuchs for the sake of the work of God, I would sincerely wish that every young widow would decide to follow Jesus and become a strong evangelist, in addition to the work they do.

The widower
A widower is usually the breadwinner before the death of his wife and would be expected to continue with his means of income, so care for widowers is not usually discussed. Many widowers end up remarrying, just as Abraham did. Except in situations where the dead wife never had children for the man, I would advise a man to stay out of remarriage and show love to his children. Jesus let us know, as we saw earlier, that

CHAPTER TWENTY ONE

some have made themselves eunuchs for the sake of the gospel of the kingdom.

Instead of remarrying and living with a woman who will give you a headache and maltreat your children, you are better off getting busy with the work of God, and showing more love to your children. Abraham's marriage to Keturah reduced the wealth meant for Isaac which Sarah had assisted Abraham to labour for, and even denied as a wife in two instances, and this would be seen in Isaac's decision to leave for Egypt during the famine in the land, in Genesis 26, after the death of his father, because Abraham had settled the children of Keturah with gifts and sent them to the east (Genesis 25:1-6).

If every man would love his children, and respect their wives even at death, they should desist from remarrying. I would buttress my argument with the fact that if Eve had died, where would Adam get another wife from, since they were alone? Would Adam have married his own daughter? Jesus gave us the clue to all these: *but from the beginning it was not so.* – Matthew 19:8.

Though God is not against remarrying, I would want every widow and widower to consider the implication of remarrying in the face of the peace, love and joy that exist in their homes with their children. The injection of another person in the name of remarriage into many homes has led to unhappiness and even to the eventual deaths of members of the existent family.

CHAPTER TWENTY ONE

It is my joy to see that you have read this book. My prayer is that God, who revealed this wisdom in this book, will stand to defend your marriage when spiritual cankerworms come visiting, In Jesus' Name. Amen.

COVENANT CONFESSION

If you are not born again, you may have read this book like a literary material and will not receive the spirit it carries. You can make a decision to correct that now by saying this covenant confession.

Lord Jesus, I know now that you died for my sins. I believe and confess you as my Lord and Saviour. Please come into my life and dwell inside of me.

If you just said this confession, you should locate a spirit filled church to fellowship with them – let the pastor know you just gave your life to Christ and you will be directed on what to do next. Salvation is a personal race and you must be serious with it.

You can also give us a call through the numbers below:
+234-8076190064; +234-8086737791.
Or send us email at:
christmovementinternational@gmail.com

BOOKS BY THE SAME AUTHOR

1. Existing In The Supernatural
2. The Altar In Golgotha
3. How Good and Large is your Land?
4. Born To Blossom

5. Battles Beyond The Physical
6. The Path To Absolute Freedom
7. The Man God Made
8. Aspects of Marriage

To contact Pastor Oghenethoja Umuteme send an email to president@christmovementinternational.org
You can join him on Facebook and Twitter also:
www.facebook.com/Pst Oghenethoja Umuteme
www.twitter.com/PstUmuteme

WORSHIP WITH US
@
ROYAL DIAMONDS INT'L CHURCH
(aka Christ Movement)
Nnata Close by Weli Street
Rumunduru/Eneka Road
Rumunduru
Port Harcourt, Nigeria
Please call or send us email to know our worship days and time.
Phone: +234-8086737791
Email: christmovementinternational@gmail.com
info@christmovementinternational.org

www.ingramcontent.com/pod-product-compliance
Lightning Source LLC
Chambersburg PA
CBHW051751040426
42446CB00007B/317